The Business Communication Workbook

Skills and Strategies for the Working World

Revised First Edition

The Business Communication Workbook

Skills and Strategies for the Working World

Written and edited by

Emily Carlson Goenner

St. Cloud State University

 cognella® | ACADEMIC PUBLISHING

Bassim Hamadeh, CEO and Publisher
Mieka Portier, Acquisitions Editor
Sean Adams, Project Editor
Jess Estrella, Senior Graphic Designer
Alisa Munoz, Licensing Associate
Natalie Piccotti, Director of Marketing
Kassie Graves, Vice President of Editorial
Jamie Giganti, Director of Academic Publishing

Cover image copyright © 2015 Depositphotos/Maverick_inanta.

Printed in the United States of America.

ISBN: 978-1-5165-9182-4 (pbk) / 978-1-5165-9183-1 (br)

CONTENTS

INTRODUCTION

1   Why Study Business Communication?

Most students reading this text will be majoring in finance, accounting, marketing, management, or another business area. Many students wonder why Business Communication is a required or recommended course in the business program, and many feel uncomfortable with the topic. Perhaps they believe themselves bad writers or bad at English after negative experiences in high school. Perhaps they, like most Americans, are nervous or uncomfortable giving oral presentations. As you will read below, research consistently demonstrates that to be successful in business, people need to have effective communication skills.

Developing or improving communication skills is often a key to getting a job and advancing in the position. People need to know how to present themselves in a professional business environment, how to share their ideas clearly and concisely in effective writing communications, and how to tell bosses, colleagues, and clients about projects, proposals, and developments.

In this book, you will learn a variety of skills to help you succeed in the workforce. This text will follow a consistent format for each section. First, there will be a short introduction to the topic, emphasizing the importance of the topic. Then, one or two articles about the topic, from outside sources, will provide detailed information, opinions, or ideas about the topic. Finally, the chapter will end with one or more Applying this Skill activities for students to complete. Depending on your instructor, you may be requested to complete an activity before class or during class. You will often work with other students in the class to apply information or practice concepts. In the text, these "Applying this Skill" activities will be clearly labeled, as will "Learning Objectives" so you always understand the reason you are being asked to complete an assignment or activity. The text also includes "Assignment" headings; these assignments are to be completed outside of class.

If an instructor has requested you purchase this text for your Business Communications course, your instructor is dedicated to creating a classroom environment that may be unusual in many business schools. This text focuses on active learning techniques that you will apply in the classroom; this means you will be practicing and applying the skills you are learning, both individually and in small groups. Most likely, you will be involved in small group discussions, peer review of documents, group brainstorming, short competitions, and learning a portion of information and sharing it with others. Research and surveys of learners consistently reveal most students learn best and retain information most effectively if they practice and apply concepts during the course.

After successful completion of this course, you will be ready to present your best self to the work world, and you, and your company, will avoid embarrassing errors like the one below:

FIGURE 1.1 Dakotas typo.

Source: http://college.usatoday.com/2015/12/29/univ-of-s-d-on-billboard-typo-it-happens/.

Reading 1.1

Employers Indentify Four "Must Have" Career Readiness Competencies for College Graduates

By NACE Staff

When asked to rate the career readiness competencies of college graduates in terms of "essential need," employers view four as vital, according to results of NACE's *Job Outlook 2016 Spring Update*.

NACE's seven career readiness competencies represent the skills, experiences, and attributes that broadly prepare students for a successful transition into the work force. (Click here for the competencies and their definitions.)

Employers deemed their top four career readiness competencies—critical thinking/problem solving, professionalism/work ethic, teamwork, and communications skills—to be between "essential" and "absolutely essential" in the college graduates they are looking to hire. (See Figure 1.2.)

These results are consistent with those posted a year ago, indicating that these competencies are virtual "must haves."

The *Job Outlook 2016 Spring Update* survey was conducted from February 10–March 22, 2016. The survey was sent to 944 NACE members; 144, or 15.3 percent, responded. NACE members can access the Job Outlook 2016 Spring Update report through MyNACE.

Competency	Essential Need Rating	
	2016	**2015**
Critical Thinking/Problem Solving	4.7	4.7
Professionalism/Work Ethic	4.7	4.5
Teamwork	4.6	4.6
Oral/Written Communications	4.4	4.4
Information Technology Application	3.9	3.9
Leadership	3.9	3.9
Career Management	3.6	3.6

FIGURE 1.2 Employers Rate Career Readiness Competencies in Terms of Essential Need (2016 vs. 2015).

Weighted average. Based on a 5-point scale where 1 = Not essential; 2 = Not very essential; 3 = Somewhat essential; 4 = Essential; 5 = Absolutely essential.

Source: National Association of Colleges and Employers, http://www.naceweb.org/career-readiness/competencies/employers-identify-four-must-have-career-readiness-competencies-for-college-graduates/.

Foundations

- ▶ Introductions
- ▶ Elements of Written Communication
- ▶ Peer Assessment and Review
- ▶ Effective Writing

I n Unit 1: Foundations, you will learn some skills that will help you throughout this course and in the world of work. At every beginning, you have to meet and get to know people. So, in this text you start with giving and making introductions. Then, you will be introduced to the 5 Cs of Communication which are elements you will apply to written and interpersonal communication throughout the course. Next, you will learn how to provide both positive and constructive feedback to others and how to examine a document. Finally, you will review your writing skills and learn some stylistic characteristics of business writing that will help you create clear and concise documents throughout the course. As is true with many textbooks, this one builds upon the basics you learn in the first unit so understanding these core concepts is vital to your success in the remainder of the course. In addition, a strong foundation is the first step to developing your effective business communication skills.

2 Introductions

Throughout your professional career, you will be introduced to and introduce other people. Each semester as you start new classes, you introduce yourself to the instructor and your fellow students. After college, you'll be new at a job, the new person on a team or at a meeting, or meeting new clients. You will have to introduce yourself and introduce other people, so learning skills to help you do so effectively will help your career.

After completing this lesson, you will:

- Understand how to properly introduce yourself and someone else
- Know how to network

Reading 2.1

Master the Secrets of Networking: *Brand You! To Land Your Dream Job*

By Diane Huth

Now that you have joined several organizations, you have to show up and participate!

Most organizations have weekly or monthly luncheons, and a couple of evening networking socials throughout the year, in addition to workshops and seminars. Some groups feature breakfast meetings, others evening dinners or cocktail events. Join organizations that fit into your lifestyle so it will be easy and convenient to attend the events. Attend whenever possible, and actively network with the others in the room.

How I Learned the Secret of Successful Networking

When I moved to San Antonio from Florida fifteen years ago, I knew nobody. I was a recently divorced single woman, and I didn't know a soul. I sat at home for a few months because I didn't know how to connect with other people. Then somebody from my homeowners' association said, "*Hey, there's a big party for a local charity this weekend; here's an invitation.*" I decided I had to change my life as I was miserable and alone and lonely, so I made up my mind to go—by myself.

I sat in the car in my evening gown outside the event center, terrified to walk into a room full of hundreds of strangers by myself. I finally got up the nerve, walked in the door, stuck out my hand and said "*Hi, I'm Diane, and I'm a new Texan.*" I repeated this introduction all night long. I met dozens of people, and everyone was friendly and welcoming. I had a wonderful time and I danced until 1:30 in the morning. Then, just the next week, I ran into a couple of those same people at a restaurant, joined them at their table, and they weren't strangers any more. All of a sudden I had a wonderful group of friends. In the years since, it has snowballed until I have a huge personal and online network of friends and business colleagues. If I had not put aside my fear (terror is more like it) and walked into that room full of strangers and started introducing myself, my life would have taken a very different course. Yours will too when you master the art of networking.

How to Work the Room at a Networking Event

The goal at networking events is to network. So don't hang around or sit with your friends or sit at a table full of students from your school or colleagues from your office. Actively seek out new people you don't know, and ask to sit with them.

Force yourself out of your comfort zone and actively seek to meet new people. Shake hands, and say *"Hi, I'm Diane, and I'm brand new here,"* or *"Hi, I'm the PR Chair for this organization and I don't think I have met you before,"* or *"Hi, I belonged to this organization in Houston, but I just moved here and am looking forward to meeting other members like you."* Then, sit at a table of strangers. Always sit at a table with people you don't know, because at the end of the event, they're going to be your friends or at least acquaintances. How are you going to meet people if you don't sit with them and talk to them? You have to force yourself out of your comfort zone and actively reach out to new people.

Master the Art of Shaking Hands

Next you have to master the all-important hand shake. No wimpy finger shakes, ladies, and no crushing of fingers, guys. When you say your name, stick out your right hand, insert your hand securely into the other person's hand thumb-to-thumb and palm-to-palm. Firmly grasp the offered hand, look the person you are greeting in the eye, smile, shake hands 3 times, then release.

To be really sincere or intimate, use the two-hand shake. Look the person in the eye, and grasp the offered hand firmly with your right hand, and then clasp the back side of the person's hand with your left hand, and shake. Release your left hand first, then release your right hand. I would recommend using this sparingly, as you don't want to be known as a groper, but it can be good for a very special person or relationship.

Wear Your Nametag on Your Right Shoulder

Nametags are essential for networking. Most organizations will have preprinted computer-generated stick-on nametags for networking events. Sometimes you will receive a blank adhesive nametag and a Sharpie pen to write your own name tag. Practice writing an attractive nametag, with your first name large and very visible, and your last name underneath a bit smaller. If you want to add your company name, it should be centered at the bottom in a smaller size printing.

Even better, you can invest $10 or $15 to create your own permanent nametag. If you currently don't have a job, list your profession instead of company—what you aspire to do. For example: Marketing, Accounting, Human Resources, Writer-Editor, IT, Database Management, Auto Repairs, etc. Don't put your school name if you are still in school. And never put intern, job seeker, or unemployed on anything!

You wear your nametag on your RIGHT shoulder, just below your collarbone, about where you would put your hand to say the pledge of allegiance on the other shoulder. You want your name tag to be seen when you introduce yourself to someone. When you stick out your right hand to shake hands, your right shoulder will roll forward, and your name tag will be clearly visible. When you shake hands, your left shoulder rolls backwards and the person you are meeting can't see your nametag well if it is on the left shoulder.

Manage Giving and Receiving Business Cards

Presenting, accepting, and managing business cards is an art. I keep my business cards in the left pocket of my jacket, always within easy reach. You don't want to be fumbling in your purse or wallet for a card—that's awkward and distracting. When I meet someone I want to give a business card to, I dip my left hand into my left pocket and pull out a card while I am reaching out with my right hand to shake hands. Then I present my card so that it is facing the recipient and not upside down. At that point, the recipient feels obligated to return the gracious gesture, and he gives me one of his cards.

Take the offered card in both hands, read it, say the name, and thank the giver for the card. Then slip it into your RIGHT side pocket. In this way, you aren't fumbling through many cards to find one of yours, and you aren't giving away a card with a hand-written note on the back. Practice this before your next networking event so it comes to you naturally. Remember, your cards in your left pocket, and their cards in your right pocket.

Business card etiquette is very different in different countries and cultures, so study up on the cultural nuances before traveling overseas.

Learn My 3-Person Rule

I have a networking rule cast in stone: every time you go out to an event of any kind, you have to meet and really connect with 3 people. You can't leave until you have spoken one-on-one with 3 people, found out where they work, what they do, what their hobbies are, how long they've belonged to the association or have been attending their events. And you have to exchange business cards—that one with your photo, remember? Three new people should be your mantra.

So every time you network, you don't need to meet everybody. You just have to really meet and get to know just 3 people. It's not overwhelming when you focus on just 3 people. At the end of the year, you will know at least 36 new people well from just one group that meets monthly. Those people will introduce you to their friends to exponentially expand your network. Then all of a sudden you will walk into a room full of friends instead of strangers.

Introduce Yourself Memorably

Most people don't know how to introduce themselves. They say their name as if is just one word. "*Hi, I'm Barbarajacobson.*" The person you are meeting can't understand what you just said. They hear "*Hi, I'm Barbara blah blah blah.*" You need to put an auditory space between your first and last name so it can be heard, processed, understood and then hopefully remembered. You have to learn that you have a new middle name and it is SPACE. So when you introduce yourself, you say, "*Hi, I'm Barbara (space) Jacobson.*" You need to practice it until it flows smoothly and naturally. There's a great TED Talk that demonstrates this: *Want to sound like a leader? Start by saying your name right*—by Laura Sicola of TEDxPenn.

Look for and try to create an auditory prompt so your name is easy to remember. If you have a name with another meaning, try using it as a memory prompt. My friend Brook Carey introduces herself by saying "*Hello, I'm Brook Carey. That's Brook like a babbling brook, and Carey like Drew Carey.*" They will remember her name because she created a rich visual image in their mind, and a visual image is stronger than just an auditory message for creating memory. I have an unusual last name, so I introduce myself on the phone as "*Hi, I'm Diane Huth—that's H-U-T-H Huth.*" In the past I tried to add, "*It's pronounced Huth—like Ruth.*" That was memorable—but everyone remembered *Ruth* instead of *Diane* and called me *Ruth*, so that didn't work out so well. Your challenge is to come up with a clever way to help a stranger remember your name, and practice your introduction until it comes naturally.

It's Important to Remember THEIR Names

You must also remember and repeat the name of the person you just met. Repeat the new person's name at least three times in the first minute after an introduction to help remember his name. Your conversation might go, "*Hi, Steve, it's nice to meet you. Steve, what do you do for a living? Steve, I want to introduce you to my friend Mary. Mary, this is Steve, Steve, this is Mary.*" At the end of this exchange, you will probably remember that his name is "*Steve.*"

My Secret Name Recall Tip

Remembering someone's name is very important in creating likeability. But sometimes you do forget. Let me share my secret trip for recalling someone's name.

For several years, I headed up both a trade organization and a singles social group, and was on the podium presenting speakers and addressing the audience at events. Many people knew my name, but I didn't know or remember theirs. Like many people, I'm awful at remembering names in the first place, so it was a real challenge for me. I created this technique that will serve you well in your career.

When someone comes up to me and says *"Hi, Diane, I haven't seen you in ages,"* I don't ask them who they are—that would be an insult. Instead I immediately shake hands and then introduce them to someone whose name I do know. The conversation might go like this: *"I'm great, thanks. I'd love to introduce you to my friend Bob."* Bob politely sticks out his hand and says *"Hi, I'm Bob Jones."* Then the new person introduces herself to Bob, saying, *"Hi, Bob, I'm Barbara Jacobson."* Aha! Now I know her name, and I can say *"Barbara, what have you been up to lately?"*

It's All About Them

When you're talking to people while you are networking, there is one golden rule: *"It's not about you, it's about them."* Being a good conversationalist doesn't mean that you talk in an enchanting or interesting manner about yourself. It means that you LISTEN to them talk about themselves! They don't care about you, quite frankly. They want to talk about themselves and you may have to prompt them to get started.

Ask them about themselves: *"How long have you belonged to this organization?" "What do you do for a living?" "How long have you worked for that company?" "That's an interesting last name—what is the origin?" "What are your biggest challenges in your job today?"* Your challenge is to get them talking about themselves, their company and their interests. As they talk, you nod and give them words or gestures and body language of encouragement or acknowledgement. They're going to think you're fascinating. Ask smart questions. Every time you ask smart questions and they answer, you should acknowledge and affirm what they say with a nod, a smile, an *"umhumm"* or a statement of interest.

My friend and mentor John Carter told me how he was hired right out of graduate school for a much sought-after job in account management with the J Walter Thompson advertising agency in New York City—a plum of a job. He had an on-campus interview with a recruiter, just like twenty other students that day. When he sat down with the recruiter, he said, *"I know what an account executive does, and I know what a copywriter does, but I don't know what Human Resources does."*

The recruiter launched into an animated explanation of how important his job was and how business was changing and how they were the frontline for acquiring talent for the company and on and on. When the half-hour interview was over, John had never talked about himself or the job or his qualifications. He left discouraged—expecting another polite rejection letter. The company extended a job offer to only one person from that campus recruiting trip. Yep, John got the job—only because he was a good listener and got the interviewer to talk about himself.

Another of my friends has not been able to find a job despite great talent and experience. I took her with me to a professional networking social, and all she did was talk about herself all night long. I was talking with somebody whom I wanted to have come and speak at a class, and every time I asked him a question, she interrupted talking about herself and how she felt about the topic. I redirected the questions to him again and again, saying, *"Brad, tell me about this,"* and every time he tried to answer, she jumped in talking about herself and her opinions and experiences. I finally had to drag her away and say, *"Shut up. It's not about you, it's about him. Let him talk about himself and don't interrupt or talk about yourself."* She didn't know how to network effectively, and never really learned, which is why she still hasn't been able to land a job. So network wisely and effectively and listen much more than you talk.

Follow Up Immediately After a Networking Event

At the end of any event, go home and send your 3 special new contacts a quick email before you go to bed. Don't wait until tomorrow or you will never get around to it. It can be something simple like *"It was such a pleasure to meet you tonight at the AMA social. I'd like to stay in touch. Perhaps we can connect on LinkedIn."* Immediately go to LinkedIn and send her an invitation. Then you can communicate and build on your relationship and set up that one-on-one meeting.

If you really are interested in the person or company, hand-write a thank you note with pen and paper. Handwriting a thank you note is an almost obsolete forgotten skill, but people respond to it, in part because they can't hit "delete" to make it go away. If you have bad handwriting, type the note nicely on a good linen paper or notecard stock, sign it and send it in the mail. The important thing is to reach out to the other person on paper, and insert or attach your business card (with your photo of course) as a tangible reminder of your meeting.

Master the Secret Art of Team Networking

One of the skills I have honed is that of Team Networking. My friend Marie is a very good graphic designer and we attend professional networking events together. When I meet someone new, I introduce them to Marie with praise. *"It's a pleasure to meet you, John. I want to introduce you to my friend, Marie. She's the best graphic designer in town. She does all of my graphic design work, and I've worked with her for ten years. I think you need to know each other."* Then Marie says *"Oh, it's so easy to do great work for someone like Diane. She is the most brilliant marketer I've*

This connection really is very powerful. You can say, *"I enjoyed hearing about your company last night. It sounds like you have fascinating opportunities. Could we get together and have a cup of coffee next week to learn more about it? I'd love to work for a company like yours."* It is that easy.

ever met. She's introduced me to the most wonderful clients. I just love working with her."

So we each bragged about each other! I didn't brag about myself, and Marie didn't brag about herself, right? But we told John a great deal of favorable information about each other. In this way I can act modest because I bring my cheering squad with me, and we both look good. Plus it's much more fun to go networking with a friend—especially if you have complementary or non-competing skills and aren't both looking for the same job.

Networking No-Nos

Some topics should be avoided at networking events. You should never talk about religion or politics. And never, ever talk negatively about anybody, including nasty people that you've worked with before or people you hate. That's private. Discussing it will make you look petty. Don't ever bring negative topics or experiences into a professional social networking event, or interview for that matter. And don't gossip or reveal secrets about a former employer, even if you left unhappily. You will be seen as being disloyal. After all, if you will tell me confidential information about your former

employer, I have to assume you would probably do the same if you end up working for my company.

> **TAKEAWAY**—Networking is your secret weapon to landing a great job. People prefer to hire people they know. So your challenge is to effectively network and meet both the people who can refer you to a job, as well as your future employer, through industry and civic associations. Network your way to your dream job!

TO DO LIST:

- Practice shaking hands effectively and smiling, while introducing yourself memorably by saying your name slowly, with a space between your first and second name
- Practice your opening line—how you introduce yourself, and what memory-stimulating device you will use
- Practice exchanging business cards, keeping your cards in your left pocket and their cards in your right pocket
- Order a permanent name tag from your local trophy shop; make a note to always wear it on your right shoulder
- Find a friend with whom you can team network

Applying This Skill: Introductions

Since introductions are essential to starting relationships, you will practice introductions.

First, everyone will get up—you have to move around the room. Introduce yourself to 3–4 people in the class. You must introduce yourself to at least two people on the other side of the classroom! Practice some introduction skills, including:

- Shaking hands
- Saying your name clearly
- Asking for and sharing details
- Starting a conversation
- Establishing your presence in the class

Second, you will pair with another student. Now, you will do a more in-depth introduction; you'll need paper and pen to take notes. Find somewhere to sit as a pair. Ask each other some of the questions below; questions with an * are required. Take notes, and be prepared to introduce your partner to the remainder of the class.

Questions:

- Name*
- Major*
- Year in school*
- Future goals
- Interesting fact about you
- Hobbies or interests
- Something unique (travel, family, personal story, pets)*
- Aspects of course you are concerned about*
- Aspects of course you are looking forward to

Each person will stand up and introduce their partner to the class. Introductions are essential to building relationships and helping people connect. This exercise helps the class begin to build a welcoming, supportive community.

3 Elements of Written Communication

In communications studies, you can learn about encoding and decoding, interference, and more, but for our purposes, you need to know, practically, the elements necessary for effective communication. The Cs of communication are an easy way to identify the major characteristics of effective communication. This will help you create and edit your written communications. After completing this lesson, you will:

- Understand the Cs of communication
- Be able to apply the Cs of communication to a written document

The 5 Cs of Communication

For our purposes, the 5Cs of communication mean your writing should be:

- Clear
- Concise
- Complete
- Consistent
- Considerate

The section below will explain, in detail, each aspect of communication.

CLEAR

Clear writing means communicating your message so the receiver understands easily. A clear message has a clear purpose, addresses the receiver's needs and questions, and is written using the following guidelines:

- Use short sentences—readers may get lost or confused by long, convoluted sentences; one idea per sentence is best.
- Use concrete words—concrete words refer to things we know through our senses; they are tangible qualities and characteristics. Abstract words refer to vague ideas or qualities and intangible characteristics.
    - Concrete: To succeed in this course, you must read the textbook, study hard, and attend class.
    - Abstract: To succeed in the course, you must work hard.
- Avoid clichés—clichés are overused words and phrases that have a general meaning or have lost their meaning; using clichés can cause confusion, misunderstandings, and unclear writing and make you seem like a lazy, unoriginal writer. Common clichés include:
    - Every cloud has a silver lining.
    - It's raining cats and dogs.
    - Get your ducks in a row.
    - All over the map
- Use appropriate and accurate words—tailor your message to the audience, and use appropriate terms (purview vs. area; pay vs. remunerate; cognizant vs. aware); use the correct version of commonly confused words (their, they're, there; affect, effect; whether, weather, etc.)
- Use appropriate facts and figures—include details, figures, data, and statistics when it will increase the clarity of your message.
- Use visual enhancements to increase readability; use bullet lists to itemize numerous tasks or points.

CONCISE

Concise writing presents a complete message as briefly as possible; use as few words as possible to get your message across clearly. Concise messages save companies time and money because no reader wants to wade through long blocks of text to find relevant information. State your point briefly and clearly. To improve conciseness, do the following:

- Avoid unnecessary repetition (completely finish, basic fundamentals, large in size).
- Avoid wordy phrases (first and foremost, in order to, point in time).
- Avoid circumlocutions (at this point in time vs. now; due to the fact that vs. because; in reference to vs. about).
- Avoid starting sentences with "It is" or "There are."
    - "There are two assignments due next week" vs. "Two assignments are due next week."
- Unneeded modifiers (really, basically, actually)
- Weak phrases (seems like, might be)

Aim to reduce the word count in your first draft by 10–20%.

COMPLETE

Complete writing means thinking of the needs of the audience. What does the audience need/want to know? What questions will the audience have? A complete message leaves the reader without any questions or need to continue a back-and-forth conversation.

Remember the 5 Ws when writing, and answer as many of these questions as possible:

- Who
- What
- Where
- When
- Why

Ensure the receiver has the information needed to take action. Include:

- Times and dates
- Order numbers
- Places

CONSISTENT

Consistency covers both content and writing details. Failure to be consistent may, at worst, confuse your readers and, at best, show lack of attention to detail. Both show a lack of professionalism.

Consistency includes broad topics like products/services, general attitude toward customers and employers, and responsiveness to messages. Maintaining consistent messaging across areas of and among employees of a company is very important on a company-wide scale.

Ensuring consistency within your own messages is no less important. Plan and organize your document to ensure your reader understands the topic and purpose. Refer to people, places, topics, etc. with the same terms throughout the document. For example, use "customer" throughout rather than alternating between "customer" and "user." Clearly define different places, accounts, times, meetings, etc.

When writing, ensure consistency in the following ways:

- Format and style (document design, use of visual enhancements, spacing, etc.)
- Citations, references, and footnotes (use of MLA, APA, or other style guidelines)
- Grammar (comma use, capitalization, numbers)
- Spelling—including use of contractions (don't vs. do not)
- Abbreviations and acronyms (Avenue vs. Ave.)

Consistency in your messages will be developed through careful planning, editing, and proofreading.

CONSIDERATE

Writing with consideration means focusing on the reader's needs, problems, desires, and questions. It is a focus on "you" (the reader/receiver) vs. a focus on "I" or "we" (the writer). As writers, we consider how readers will respond to our messages, anticipating their emotional reactions and potential questions/concerns.

Consideration is largely about the tone of your message. Who are you writing to? Is it a formal or informal audience? Does your writing target that audience?

- Use "you attitude"—("Your order will arrive in 3–5 days" vs. "We sent your order this morning").
- Write positively—emphasize the positive, demonstrate benefits.
- Be tactful, thoughtful, polite—choose words carefully to be pleasant and respectful.
- Avoid discriminatory terms (manpower vs. workers/employees; server vs. waitress).

Writing with consideration will enhance goodwill, increase trust, and contribute to a positive business relationship.

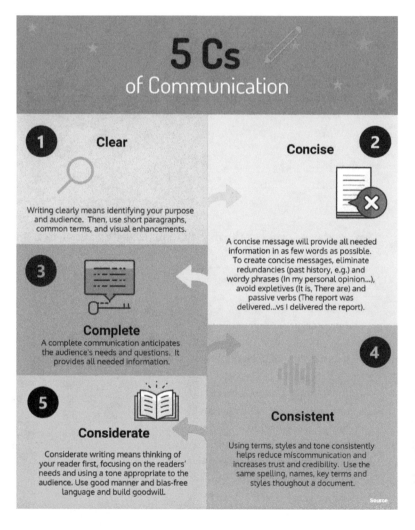

FIGURE 3.1 5 Cs of Communication.

Applying This Skill: 5 Cs of Communication Exercise

The class will be divided into five groups; each group will be assigned a "C" of communication. In order to develop an understanding of the 5 Cs of Communication, work as a group to apply your assigned "C" to the paragraph below. How does your assigned "C" apply to this paragraph? Is it used? Should it be applied? How?

Be prepared to explain your "C" and share your work with the class.

Someone called from the customer that we sent the big Shipment to, saying that they were having a problem with some of our product. The caller thought that there was probably going to be some more information heading our way pretty soon. They indicated that they were really concerned because this is not the first time this has happened. It might be fairly costly to them if something isn't done soon to take care of this problem. This might be a "no brainer" if the problem is the same as it was the last time we got on the "bad side" of this customer. We all know what a pain they can be when they don't get what they want. We have heard this song and dance before about them taking their business elsewhere. But we all know that the Customer is always right, and we will need to jump through any hoops they want us to in order to keep their business. If we don't hear something by the p.m., we will know the "ax" is going to fall on someone either here or in HQ.*

* Paragraph adapted from 50 Communication Activities, Icebreakers and Exercises by Peter R. Garber

4   Peer Assessment and Review

One of the most important skills needed in the workplace is how to communicate positive and negative feedback to others. Feedback is important for learning, insight, and growth. In your position, you will most likely have to give feedback to employees, peers, clients, and others. You may have to write performance reviews or give verbal feedback, either formally or informally.

One way to think of feedback is as a gift. You're helping the other person improve. Think of both giving and receiving feedback as a growth opportunity, but both giving and receiving feedback can be hard. When giving feedback, you may not feel qualified to make reliable judgments or provide insightful comments on another person's work or performance. You may be afraid to comment for a variety of reasons, including fear of hurting the other person's feelings and negative repercussions for you. Despite these fears, studies show students make judgments and comments similar to ones their professors would make. You are qualified to give feedback.

In this lesson, you will learn how to give feedback. You will think about positive and negative feedback in your life and then learn about the process of editing and revising written documents.

After completing this lesson, you will be able to:

- Deliver effective feedback
- Use the editing and revising process
- Identify common proofreader's marks

Feedback

Peer feedback activities help develop critical thinking and reflection skills, which employers sometimes say are lacking in new hires. Peer feedback helps develop sensitivity to how you say something and the impact of your words, and it helps you accept and respond to criticism. If you get multiple opinions, you may value the feedback more than if only one person makes a comment. Ultimately, everyone makes mistakes; learning to respond is important to developing resiliency.

POSITIVE FEEDBACK

Think about how often you give positive feedback to coworkers, other students, friends, or family members. Do you give positive feedback daily? Weekly? Occasionally? Never? Think about in what situations you give positive feedback. Is it a work situation, when you praise a coworker? Do you find giving praise natural, or is it something you have to work at? If you rarely give positive feedback, why? What stops you from praising others?

Praise encourages people to keep doing a task. If your supervisor hands out minutes from a staff meeting and you mention how helpful that is to your project, your supervisor is likely to keep distributing meeting minutes. Praise increases confidence, performance, and motivation.

CRITICAL FEEDBACK

While positive feedback feels good, negative feedback can have an even bigger impact on a person's emotional state and job performance. Critical feedback may feel like a personal attack, unjustified or untrue. Think of a time when you received negative feedback. Was it hurtful or helpful? Why? What made it hurtful? Was it recent or a long time ago? A majority of adults report feeling extremely hurt when receiving negative feedback, which has lasting effects on relationships and job performance.

Is it possible to give feedback in useful, helpful, and less harsh ways? Of course! Most people will respond better to feedback that is valid, reliable, fair, and useful and when it is delivered as constructive criticism. Feedback is useful when it focuses on solutions or alternatives and when it is honest and tactful. Constructive, positive feedback can help build relationships and trust, improve job performance, and promote professional development. Completing the following readings and activities should help your class develop a common vocabulary for giving positive, constructive feedback.

Applying This Skill: Tips on Giving Constructive—Not Destructive—Feedback

Business Writing that Builds Relationships, Syntax Training

By Lynn Gaertner-Johnson

As a group, look at the list below.

Of the twenty tips below, ten should begin with the word "Don't"; ten should not. Cross out the word "Don't" if it doesn't belong at the beginning of the tip. If it does belong, circle it.

How could you rephrase these items?

1. Don't exaggerate.

2. Don't be cute or clever.

3. Don't make a sincere, positive comment before constructive comments.

4. Don't try to balance the positives and negatives.

5. Don't equate rudeness with straight talk.

6. Don't avoid the pronouns "you" and "your" in constructive comments.

7. Don't act dense.

8. Don't be specific.

9. Don't be a hit-and-run critic.

10. Don't avoid the word "but" after a compliment.

11. Don't provide suggestions or offer to provide them.

12. Don't copy other people on constructive feedback.

13. Don't be sure your correction is valid when you correct other people's work.

14. Don't assume someone else has a problem you can help to fix.

15. Don't comment if it is not your job to do so and you have not been asked or paid for an opinion.

16. Don't focus on the future.

17. Don't counterattack.

18. Don't put your feedback in context.

19. Don't give feedback when it is too late to incorporate.

20. Don't give constructive feedback privately.

Business Writing that Builds Relationships. © *Syntax Training, Lynn Gaertner-Johnston.*

Reading 4.1

Edit, Rewrite, and Refine: *Follow the Three Stage Editing Process*

By Jack Appleman

Follow the Three-Stage Editing Process

Editing can be divided into three major focus areas:

1. message
2. organization
3. mechanics.

In the three stages of editing, each area is addressed separately because it's impossible to pay close attention to all three at the same time. Let's look at the three stages.

Message

Editing should begin with the message because it makes no sense to waste time reorganizing or reviewing the mechanics of text that isn't conveying your points clearly.

To review the clarity of your message, ask yourself a few simple questions. These questions are similar to the ones you asked when you started writing the document (Step 2: Know Where You're Taking Your Readers):

> ## Pointer
> ———————
>
> Editing is a three-stage process that focuses separately on *message*, *organization*, and *mechanics*.

Jack E. Appleman, "Edit, Rewrite, and Refine," *10 Steps to Successful Business Writing*, pp. 123-128. Copyright © 2008 by Association for Talent Development (ATD). Reprinted with permission.

- Is the purpose or bottom line clear?
- Is the action required of the reader clear?
- Are the other important points clear?
- Is the tone appropriate for the message?
- Is the message written in a positive (rather than negative) way?

As you answer those questions, mark any text you're not satisfied with (for example, a confusing action step).

Organization

All documents, even those with just a few paragraphs, need to be organized so that the reader can follow the text easily. The second stage of editing takes a hard look at how well you've imposed a logical order on the message you're trying to convey.

Here are some questions to ask yourself to determine if your document is properly organized:

- Is information separated into chunks that are easy to digest?
- Are those chunks arranged in a logical sequence?
- Does each paragraph contain just one basic idea so readers won't get confused?
- Are there transitions unifying sentences, paragraphs, and sections to help ideas in the document flow smoothly from start to finish?
- Is the structure reasonably similar throughout different sections?
- Could subheads before key sections make it easier to read?

One method to separate and arrange your ideas is to read the document and list all the key points it conveys. In essence, you're re-outlining it. This is much easier when you're looking at text you've written than it is when you're staring at a blank page. The re-outlining process also will help identify any important concepts that you omitted. You can list them separately at the bottom of the page or on a separate sheet of paper

Mechanics

Most of the grunt work in editing comes in the third stage: reviewing the mechanics of your text. Mechanics form the micro level of the document, not the macro message or the mid-level organization. Mechanics are the weeds!

On a paper copy, circle or highlight a group of words or sentences that may need revision. If you prefer editing only on a screen, use the highlighting feature or put that block of text in a different color.

Go through the entire document, marking places you may revise, before you begin revising. You may want to go through it two or three times. Then work on clarifying your message in each of the places you've marked.

and incorporate them as you reorganize the document. You'll also be able to spot repeated or similar ideas scattered throughout the document and then merge them into a single paragraph or section.

If you developed an initial outline before you started your first draft, compare that version to the re-outline to see if you omitted anything you initially intended to include.

During this stage, you may decide to change the order in which ideas are presented so they flow more logically from one to the next.

Consider adding subheads or a few words before each section (set in bold or italic, perhaps underlined) to pinpoint the key message that follows and to further separate each concept. (See Step 6 for more discussion of subheads.)

Good organization is a more subjective quality than are the message and proper mechanics. For example, the same information can be conveyed through shorter or longer paragraphs. And you can explain a multifaceted concept by using bullets to list the facets or by writing a few traditional paragraphs with no bulleted items.

When you get comfortable with your own method of organizing, you'll find that it not only promotes readability but also simplifies your writing process because you can move text around into separate categories more confidently—and get the document done faster.

Editing for mechanics—spelling, punctuation, grammar, and word usage—may require you to be in a different frame of mind than you are when evaluating message clarity and organization. You need to scrutinize individual words or groups of words instead of the entire document. Here are some questions you need to ask:

- Spelling/typos
    - Are any words misspelled?
    - Are any homonyms (sound-alikes, such as *there* and *their*) used in place of the correct words?
    - Are any words missing or out of place in a sentence?
    - Have you placed apostrophes correctly?
    - Are all proper names spelled correctly?
- Punctuation
    - Do all of your sentences end with appropriate punctuation?
    - Are all commas and periods placed inside quotation marks?
    - Do commas separate all the items in a series?
    - Do semicolons separate all the items in a comma-separated series?
- Grammar and syntax
    - Do subjects and verbs agree in number?
    - Do nouns and pronouns agree in number?
    - Is text written in a consistent tense?
    - Are sentences written in a parallel structure?
    - Are bulleted or numbered lists written in a parallel structure?
    - Are subheads written in a parallel structure?
    - Does each introductory phrase directly relate to the noun that immediately follows it?
    - Is everything written in complete sentences, where appropriate?
    - Are there short, choppy sentences that can be combined for better flow?
- Word usage
    - Is there any stuffy language that can be replaced with simpler words?

- Are there any weak passive verbs or verb-nouns that can be replaced with more powerful active verbs?
- Can you eliminate any redundant language?
- Is there jargon or "business-speak" that can be simplified with more widely understood terminology?

You can start with the spelling/grammar-checking feature usually available with word-processing software. It helps catch obvious mistakes—but *don't* depend on it. The spelling-check feature won't catch homonyms you've used incorrectly (*here, hear; do, due; there, their, they're*); and if you've written *is* when you meant *in*, the software won't catch your mistake. As to the grammar-checking feature, sometimes the software's suggestions are just plain wrong.

Another way to find mistakes is to read your words aloud in a staccato, syllable-by-syllable rhythm so you actually can hear the errors. For example, when sounding out "Lu-pé out-lined four-teen work-flow im-prove-ments is her re-port," you'll probably notice that "is" should be "in." Also try reading the text backward, forcing yourself to review one word at a time instead of getting mesmerized by the flow of sentences and paragraphs.

Editing for mechanics can be handled in many ways. You can print out your document, write your revisions on the paper copy, and then key them into the electronic file. Or you can use the tracking/redlining feature of your word-processing program, which will enable you to keep your original version without interrupting the flow of the newer version. With time, you'll discover the system that works best for you.

Applying This Skill: Peer Review Exercise

Writing is a process and requires multiple revisions to ensure a polished product. Every writer needs an editor, often more than one. In this class, you will be asked to provide feedback on other students' work. To prepare you for that task, please read about the three-step approach below. Then edit the document below; the checklist appears on the following page. You will share and compare your review with a classmate.

Three-step approach

1. Read first. Judge later. Read the piece all the way through without making marks or comments. Focus on what the writer is trying to say. Is the content clear?
2. Read again and edit. Read the piece again, highlighting sections for discussion and recording comments/questions. Mark grammatical errors or awkward wording.
3. Complete the checklist. Review the document with the related checklist.

Assess Your Document Here   **Business Letter Format & Editing Checklist**

☐⟶ Sender's Address Here
      Street Name
      City, State, Zip Code

☐⟶ Date Here

☐⟶ Addressee's Name here
      Address Here
      City, State, Zip Code

☐⟶ Salutation Here:

☐⟶ Introduction Paragraph: Open with the main idea (deductive approach). Include reason for writing and outline of information to follow in the document (outline statement).

☐⟶ Body paragraph 1: Start with topic sentence. Include supporting information. Use specific details and in-text citations when appropriate.

☐⟶ Body paragraph 2: Use basic body paragraph organization. Use visual enhancements and design elements as needed, including bullets, bold, italics, and subheadings. Remember and apply the Cs of Communication.

☐⟶ Body paragraph (if needed):

☐⟶ Conclusion: Provide a sense of closure. Remind reader of main point; include action steps if needed. Include a forward-looking statement and include contact statement (who reader should contact for more information).

☐⟶ Complementary Close,

☐⟶ Signature here

☐⟶ Sender's Name
      Sender's Title, if appropriate

☐⟶ Enclosure Notation, if needed

To: Professor Goenner, Herberger Business School, Herberger Business School, Marketing & Business Law Department, St. Cloud State University, 720 4th Avenue South, St. Cloud, MN 56301

Hello Professor, my name is Gary Johnson. I am a student at St. Cloud State University. I graduated high school Albert Lea Minnesota in 2012. While attending there I also played hockey.

At St. Cloud State University I am currently pursuing a degree in accounting; I have completed my minor in mass communications. Upon coming to SCSU I didn't know what to study, so I decided on physics because I wanted to know how the world works. I always make the joke that this is the reason I am in accounting; I studied physics because I wanted to know what makes the world turn... I ended up in accounting because I discovered what actually makes the world turn. With in that journey I picked up a minor in mass communications because there was a short time that I thought I was going to major in it after changing from physics.

Currently I work at House of Pizza in Sartell as a delivery guy; I work there about 20 hrs a week. As I attend school I hope to build the skills to eventually become a CPA and work for a firm. I hope to work my way up the ranks and eventually become a partner at a firm. I don't individually do much volunteer work, but I am a member of Delta Sigma Pi and through that we have volunteered for things like Feed my Starving Children and Highway clean-up. Being a member of DSP has benefited me in many ways including networking and communication skills. Throughout school I have developed strong oral communication skills. I hope that it will play into my favor in the future working with different clients. I am assuming non face to face interactions will also be a huge part of the position I hope to attain. That is definitely a skill I hope to improve.

An excellent example of a professional in my hopeful field of choice is my second uncle Steve Johnson. I am uncertain the firm he worked for, but he has just recently retired as a CPA after 35 years of work. Last time I talked to him he mentioned that he himself graduated from SCSU decades ago. At the family reunion I talked to him at he said to me, "I haven't worked a day in my life for 35 years. I got paid to talk business with my friends." Although I had already decided my major before talking to him, hearing that only cemented my plan for the future.

Applying This Skill: Proofreading Symbol Matching

Proofreaders and editors use a standard set of marks when editing papers. While you're not required to use those marks, your instructor may. To ensure you understand the suggestions and comments made on your writing, complete the exercise below.

Match the symbol with its standard proofreader's meaning.

1. _____ Insert period		a. trans
2. _____ Insert		b. ∧
3. _____ Insert comma		c. ≡
4. _____ Awkward construction		d. ⊙
5. _____ Insert apostrophe		e. □
6. _____ Delete		f. �
7. _____ Comma splice		g. agr
8. _____ Referent unclear		h. sp
9. _____ Wrong word		i. w
10. _____ Paragraph		j. awk
11. _____ Capitalize		k. ^
12. _____ Lower case		l. cs
13. _____ Informal or inaccurate vocabulary		m. ....
14. _____ Spell out		n. ww
15. _____ Transpose		o. /
16. _____ stet (let original stand)		p. ?
17. _____ Spelling error		q. ⩗
18. _____ Wordy		r. ‖
19. _____ What?		s. tr ∿
20. _____ Align		t. ¶
21. _____ Agreement error		u. ⌗
22. _____ Need transition		v. ref
23. _____ Space		w. v

5 Effective Writing

Every time you share a written document, you are representing yourself and the company. While most people will excuse one typographical or proofreading error in a document, multiple errors look bad, both for you and your company. Poor written communication can cause confusion and reduced efficiency, lower employee morale, and reduce creativity. Errors in policy, for example, can hamper business efforts, while mistakes in marketing materials may affect customer/client relationships. Errors make you appear unprofessional and sloppy, with a lack of attention to detail. Customers or clients may wonder if you will treat them with the same lack of concern. So the details of writing and proofreading are important.

Do you believe a comma cost one company $10 million? Or that a typo and one missing letter ruined a company?

Reading 5.1

The $10 Million Comma

How one law that was missing a comma cost a company $10 million.

By Mignon Fogarty

People have such strong opinions about the Oxford comma that in 2013 the satire site The Onion published an article titled "4 Copy Editors Killed in Ongoing AP Style, Chicago Manual Gang Violence," which ended by lamenting an innocent bystander who committed suicide after being "caught up in a long-winded dispute over use of the serial, or Oxford, comma."

But that little comma before the *and* in a series like *red*, *white*, and *blue* is no joke for contract lawyers. Last week, news broke that the Oakhurst Dairy in the state of Maine would have to pay its milk-truck drivers approximately $10 million because of a missing serial comma in Maine's overtime law.

In this class action case, the two sides were arguing about the duties employees do for which they *don't* get overtime pay. This is the ambiguous sentence that describes the exemptions:

The canning, processing, preserving, freezing, drying, marketing, storing, packing for shipment or distribution of:

1. Agricultural produce;
2. Meat and fish products; and
3. Perishable good.

The drivers do distribute perishable goods—milk—but the important part is that there is no comma after the word *shipment* in the phrase *packing for shipment* or *distribution,* therefore the drivers argued that the word *distribution* is modifying packing and isn't a separate thing that makes them exempt.

In other words, the drivers said, "We don't package milk" so we aren't exempt from overtime pay, and the dairy said, "Wait a minute, you distribute perishable goods, so you are exempt." And this all rests on how you interpret the final part without a serial comma: *packing for shipment* or *distribution of … perishable goods.*

Complicating matters is that Maine Legislative Drafting Manual tells lawmakers not to use serial commas—an outrage if you ask me because as the court decision pointed out, the addition of a serial comma would have made the meaning absolutely clear: it would have clearly marked *distribution* as a separate activity.

Instead, lawmakers left it out.

The Maine Manual actually warns lawmakers about sentences just like the one in question—where a list item is modified, and it says that instead of trying to solve the problem with a comma, they should rewrite the entire sentence so they don't need one.

But they didn't, which left the dairy and the drivers with an ambiguous sentence. Worth $10 million.

An earlier court ruled in favor of the dairy, but now the United States Court of Appeals for the First Circuit has overturned that ruling in favor of the drivers. Circuit Judge David J. Barron wrote the opinion, which is more pleasant to read than most court documents I've seen, opening "For want of a comma, we have this case."

There's a long section in the middle about whether the words *shipment* and *distribution* are synonyms, and then we get to a grammatical argument: that each of the words that describes an exempt activity—*canning, processing, preserving,* and so on—are gerunds, but *shipment* and *distribution* are both nouns.

Ah ha!" said the drivers. This means *shipment* and *distribution* both serve the same function, and it's a function that is different from the gerunds, also known as the exempt activities. They argue that if distribution of perishable goods were an exempt activity, it would have been called distributing perishable goods. And the court agreed. Boom. $10 million.

This isn't the first time a court case has hinged on a comma either. Back in 2006, a Canadian company lost a million-dollar case that came down to a comma before a modifying phrase.

As the Maine Legislative Drafting Manual noted, "Commas are probably the most misused and misunderstood punctuation marks in legal drafting and, perhaps, the English language. Use them thoughtfully and sparingly," and I would add "use them with extreme caution when modifying phrases are involved and millions of dollars could be at stake."

Below, you will find more articles about the cost of bad writing and the principles of professional writing. Following the articles, a series of exercises will help you develop and polish your writing skills. After completing this lesson, you will be able to:

- Evaluate and assess your current writing abilities
- Demonstrate the ability to write concisely and clearly
- Select vocabulary appropriate for the situation
- Use pronouns, numbers and parallelism
- Distinguish between and use active and passive voice

Reading 5.2

How a Missing 'S' Killed a 134-Year-Old Company

Court rules in Taylor & Sons' favor

By Kate Seamons

There are bad typos and there are *bad typos*. This story is a case of the latter. Taylor & Sons is a Welsh engineering firm founded in 1875; on Feb. 20, 2009, Companies House, the UK agency that incorporates and dissolves limited companies, listed it as being "wound up," essentially in liquidation. Except it wasn't: Taylor & Son was the company having issues. Even though the error was rectified on Feb. 23, Taylor & Sons says that the erroneous info had already been sold to credit reference agencies. Customers spotted the notice, didn't catch the missing S, and started abandoning the firm, which at the time boasted 250 employees. Among the customers who fled: Tata Steel, which had been paying the firm about $600,000 a month, per the BBC.

The *Telegraph* reports that owner Philip Davison-Sebry said that within three weeks' time, all 3,000 of its suppliers had contacted the company about terminating orders or canceling credit. The company went into administration within two months of the typo, the business having been damaged "so as to become of no real value," he says. And so Davison-Sebry sued Companies House. In a ruling Monday, a High Court judge agreed with Davison-Sebry, noting that Companies House was obligated to take reasonable care when recording such "winding ups" to verify that the correct company was being named. And while Companies House argued that the three-day lifespan of the error was too short to cause the Taylor & Sons' failure, the judge disagreed. Davison-Sebry sued for roughly $13.3 million; the BBC reports the preliminary ruling didn't address damages.

Reading 5.3

Fundamentals of Professional Writing

By Janet Mizrahi

Whether you are a student about to step into the world of work or a more seasoned employee with years of experience, you must be able to communicate effectively to advance your career. Employers consistently rank good communication skills—speaking with customers and colleagues, presenting information, and writing—in the top tier of desired skills for both new hires and current employees. The ability to concisely and accurately convey meaning to different people is a prerequisite in today's fast-paced world.

Writing like a professional—whether the document is printed or on the screen—is best taken on as a process, with careful attention paid to detail. This chapter will describe how to break down all writing tasks into a series of steps to streamline the process as well as describe the characteristics that all professional writing should embody.

Writing as a Process

Many people think that good writing flows out of the brain, into the fingers, and onto the page or screen. Nothing could be further from the truth. Professional writers know that writing, like any acquired skill, requires patience and persistence. Whatever we are composing—whether an e-mail message or a proposal for a new business—the key to writing well is to consider writing a process rather than a one shot deal. Your prose will be better and will take you less time to compose if you look at writing as a series of tasks. For those who suffer from writer's block or who shudder at the thought of writing, I can promise that if you break down writing into several component parts, the result will be better and you will feel less anxious.

The task of writing can be broken down to three separate steps, for which I've developed an acronym: **AWE**, short for assess, write, and edit. These three steps should be completed for every piece of writing that will be seen by another person. The only writing that doesn't require this process is personal writing.

Step 1: Assess

Before you ever put your fingers on the keyboard or put pen to paper, begin by assessing the writing situation and define your **audience and purpose**. I advise making this step formal: Write down your answers.

Knowing the audience—your reader—is imperative for successful writing. Writers need to be very clear about the end user because the language and style we use depends upon who will read what we write. In essence, we have to psych out the reader to accomplish our writing goal. We cannot do that unless we analyze the reader accurately.

Define the characteristics of your reader as is shown in Table 1.1:

Begin the audience analysis portion of the first stage of the writing process (assessing) by completing an audience profile template, using the criteria mentioned in Table 1.1.

The next part of assessing the writing situation is defining your **purpose**. The reason or purpose for writing in the professional world falls into three basic categories: informing, persuading, or requesting. Informative writing is a large category that includes generalized information, instructions, notifications, warnings, or clarifications. Persuasive writing makes an impression, influences decisions, gains acceptance, sells, or recommends. Requests are written to gain information or rights and to stimulate action.

Unless you define the desired outcome of the written task, you cannot possibly achieve that task's objective. Are you writing an e-mail in response to a customer complaint? Are you using social media to generate traffic to a website selling nutritional supplements? You must be clear about what you want your words to accomplish before you write.

Sometimes you do not have all the information on hand that you need to write your document. Once you have defined for whom you are writing and what you

TABLE 1.1 Audience profile template

Audience characteristic	Rationale
Age	Writing for children differs from writing for adults or teens. Your tone, word choice, and medium may differ greatly depending on the age of the reader.
Gender	Writing for an all-male audience will differ from writing for an all-female audience. Likewise, if the audience is mixed, you may make different language choices than you do for a homogeneous group.
Language proficiency	The reader's knowledge of English will affect your word choice, sentence length, and other stylistic elements.
Education level	You may be writing for an audience with a 10th grade reading level or one comprised of college graduates. Each audience will have different expectations and needs, both of which you as the writer must be aware.
Attitude toward writer or organization	You must know if the audience is skeptical, frightened, pleased, or hostile toward you, the topic, or the organization. Anticipate your audience's reaction so you can write in a way that will support the document's purpose.
Knowledge of the topic	A document may be geared to people who are experts in a field or who know nothing about it. Even within an organization, several different audiences will exist. You may emphasize different aspects of a topic depending upon the readers' knowledge level.
Audience action	What do you want your audience to do after reading? Click a link for more information? Call to take advantage now? You must have a clear vision of your goal in communicating for your writing to be effective.

want to accomplish, continue your analysis of the writing situation by gathering the information to produce the document. Sometimes that will entail conducting **research**. Sometimes you may just need to download information from your experience. Either way, have your information on hand *before* you begin to write. Nothing is more frustrating than being on a deadline to compose a writing job and realizing that you do not have the information you need.

Once you have the information, **organize** it. For shorter pieces, think about the organizational structure you need to follow to attain your writing purpose. We will discuss these writing strategies in greater detail in Section 2. For longer pieces, begin by creating categories of information. From these sections, draft an **outline** with headings.

This assessing portion of the writing process will make the actual writing much easier. Why? It is always easier to begin writing if you have something on the page rather than nothing.

Step 2: Write

Enter the second step of the writing process—writing a draft—knowing that it is not the last step. A draft by definition is not final. Its purpose is to transfer the information you have gathered onto the page. For short documents such as routine e-mails, consider composing offline. (It's too tempting to write and hit send without carefully going over your draft!) Begin by including the information you've gathered, making sure you include each point. For longer documents, use your out-

line. Write section by section, point by point. If you have trouble with one section, move to another.

Your goal at this stage of the writing process for both short and longer documents is to put something down on paper (or the screen) that you will revise later. It's a waste of your valuable time to labor over any individual word or sentence as you write your draft; the word or sentence may be eliminated by the final version. If you cannot think of the precise word you need, leave a blank and return later to fill it in. If you are having difficulty wording a sentence smoothly, leave a bracketed space or perhaps type a few words as a reminder of the gist of what you want to say. The important point to remember is that a first draft is one of several stabs you'll take at this work.

If you write using information you have taken from other sources, avoid using someone else's words or ideas without attributing them. **Plagiarism** occurs when you use or closely imitate the ideas or language of another author without permission. Even if you paraphrase through rewording, you should still cite the source to avoid plagiarizing. With the abundance of material available to us with a few keystrokes, it's tempting to cut and paste and call it a day. But you leave yourself and your organization open to criminal liability for copyright infringement laws if you use words, images, or any other copyrighted material. Besides, you will never learn to express yourself if you use others' words.

Before you move to the next step, I advise printing your draft. But don't read it immediately. Let it marinate. It's too hard to edit our own copy immediately after we've written it. We need to let some time pass before we return to a draft so that we can be more objective when we edit.

Step 3: Edit

I saw a great T-shirt at a meeting for the Society for Technical Writers. On the front was the word *write* in bold type. Following that was line after line of the word *edit*. The final boldface word at the end of the last line was *publish*. Of course, the idea is that writing requires more editing than writing.

Editing is a multistepped process and begins by looking at the overall effectiveness of the piece. As you read your draft, return to your audience and purpose analysis and ask yourself if the content meets the needs of the audience while it accomplishes your purpose in writing. Does the document provide all the information readers will need to do what you want? Does it make sense? Is it well organized? If not, go back and make changes.

Once you are certain that the content is correct and complete, it's time for **paragraph and sentence level editing**. This is where you'll need a good style guide (see discussion of Writing Tools), unless you are one of the few who have perfect recall of all grammatical rules. Begin by examining the effectiveness of each paragraph. By definition, a paragraph is a group of sentences about one topic; the topic is generally stated in the first sentence of a paragraph and is called a topic sentence. Good paragraphs have **unity**, which means they stay on topic, so first check each paragraph for unity. Make sure your paragraphs aren't too long. Long paragraphs scare readers off.

Next check your paragraphs for **cohesion**, meaning that each sentence leads logically to the next. A common writing error is to jump from one idea to the next without providing a logical connection between those two ideas. Unless each idea expressed in a sentence logically segues to the next, your reader will not be able to follow. Writers link ideas several ways:

1. Using transitional words and phrases. Transitions are broken down into types: adding information, contrasting information, comparing information, illustrating a point, and showing time.
2. Using pronouns that refer back to a specific noun.
3. Repeating keywords to remind a reader of a central idea.

Table 1.2 illustrates the types of transitions writers use to compose cohesive sentences and paragraphs.

TABLE 1.2 Types of transitions

Type of transition	Words or phrases used
Additive—used to augment an idea	additionally, again, also, and, in addition, moreover, thus
Contrast—used to show how ideas differ	although, but, conversely, however, instead, on the other hand, yet
Comparison—used to link similar ideas	likewise, similarly
Time—used to show a sequence	after, finally, first, in the meantime, later, next, second, soon

Once all paragraphs are edited, examine each sentence. Now is the time to nitpick grammar and stylistic elements. Pay special attention to egregious errors such as:

1. Subject and verb agreement
2. Comma splices
3. Sentence fragments
4. Run-on sentences
5. Dangling modifiers

Find every pronoun to make sure it agrees with its antecedent and that the noun to which it refers is clear. Make sure you have written numbers in the correct way, using numerals and spelling out numbers appropriately. Stay in the same verb tense.

Also beware of dangling modifiers, phrases that confuse readers by saying something other than what is meant. They often appear in an introductory phrase at the beginning of a sentence but omit a word that would clarify meaning in the second part of the sentence. Look at the following sentence:

After finishing the copy, the website was difficult to understand.

The website did not finish the copy; therefore the meaning is obscure. Perhaps the sentence should have read:

After finishing the copy, the writer found that the website was difficult to understand.

As you edit, take some time to **read** your document **aloud** and make marks next to areas that require editing. This is the single best way to improve your writing. Professional writing should sound natural. If you find yourself stumbling as you read your copy, the chances are good that you have a problem; your ears will not allow you to pass over stylistic elements that your eye will just ignore. Listen for frequent repetition of the same word, for short, choppy sentences, and for sentences that begin with the same word or phrase. Make sure your sentences have variety in length, aiming for a good mix of short, medium, and longer sentences. Note whether you have started too many sentences with *there is, there are, this is,* or *it is.* Overuse of this wordy construction is a red alert for any professional writer to rewrite. Finally, make sure you have used words according to their actual definition, called the denotation. (Use the Avoiding Wordiness Checklist at the end of this chapter to help you edit for conciseness.)

The final element of the editing portion of the writing process is **proofreading**. Proofreading includes editing your copy for spelling, capitalization, punctuation, and typos. Begin by double-checking the correct spelling of names. Then make sure you've correctly used words that are commonly mistaken (i.e., affect and effect, complimentary and complementary). If you have included a phone number or a URL in the content, determine both are correct by phoning or checking the link.

A warning about using your word processor's spell check function: Spell check is far from fail proof. Just the omission of one letter (say the last *s* in *possess*) can change the word's meaning, and the program won't pick that up. *Posses* is a word (the plural of posse) but it isn't the word you meant to use. Additionally, a spell-checker won't find names spelled incorrectly or words not in its dictionary.

Proofreading for punctuation is critical. Proper use of commas makes a huge difference in a document's readability. Be especially on the lookout for inserting commas after introductory phrases and between two independent clauses joined by a coordinate conjunction. Likewise, tossing in a comma or semicolon haphazardly or omitting a comma or semicolon are common writing errors that affect readability. Both can affect flow and meaning. Consider how the comma alters these two sentences:

That, I'm afraid, has not been the case.
That I'm afraid has not been the case.

The first sentence refers to a previous statement and conveys the meaning that an earlier statement is untrue. The second means that the individual claims to be unafraid.

Capitalization is another part of the proofreading stage. Use your style guide to know when to capitalize nouns and titles and be consistent. Next examine the appearance of what you've written. Remember that copy must not only be well written; it must look attractive on the page or screen to maximize readability. You may find the Editing and Proofreading Checklist at the end of this chapter a helpful tool to guide you through this portion of the writing process.

[...]

Professional Writing Characteristics

Writing for the world of work has certain characteristics that form the underpinning of anything you write, from an e-mail to your boss, to a resume for a new job, to a proposal for new business. Integrate the following elements into your work.

Accuracy

One of the best ways we can illustrate to our readers that we are professionals and experts is through accuracy. Inaccuracies show a carelessness that few professionals or organizations can afford in a competitive, global marketplace. Attention to accuracy is therefore paramount to professionals.

Active Voice

To enliven your prose, avoid using passive voice construction when you can. Passive voice makes the object of an action the subject of a sentence, as the following example illustrates:

Passive voice	*The e-mail was written by me.*
Active voice	*I wrote the website.*

However, if you wish to obscure the person committing an action, you *should* use passive voice. You do so by avoiding naming the actor, as is illustrated below:

Passive voice	*The students were given poor grades.*
Active voice	*The professor gave the students poor grades.*

If you have trouble identifying your own use of *passive* voice, you can adjust the Grammar Tools in Microsoft Word's Preferences, which when activated, will point out passive voice construction. If you are using passive voice purposefully because you want to sound objective, great. But if you have used passive voice unintentionally, change it.

Avoiding Gender, Racial, or Age Bias

English doesn't make biases easy to avoid. The best way to stay away from the he or she conundrum is to use the plural of a word. To avoid racial or age biases, beware of stereotypes when composing. Even if you feel the reference is complimentary, those to whom you refer may find that reference offensive.

Clarity

If a reader has to reread to understand anything you write, you have not done your job. Every sentence you write that another person will see should be easy to read. Clarity comes from using words the audience will recognize and using them correctly. Stay away from jargon or SAT-prep vocabulary. One way to check your work for clarity is to give your draft to someone who knows nothing about what you are writing. If that reader can understand the document, it is probably clear.

Conciseness

Busy professionals are impatient and expect brevity. No one wants to wade through wordy prose to get to a point. As mentioned earlier, the Avoiding Wordiness Checklist at the end of this chapter contains some tips to make your writing more concise.

Conversational Prose with Smooth Flow

The rhythm of any prose needs to be conversational and natural. The best way to achieve good flow is to read your document aloud and keep amending until you are able to read without hesitation. Use simple, plain language in sentences that are not complex or convoluted. Make sure your punctuation does not *impede* your reader by adding unnecessary halts or by avoiding pauses that will aid understanding.

To make your prose more conversational, you can also use contractions when appropriate. Instead of *they will*, use *they'll*. You can also begin your sentences with *and* or *but*, which many English teachers taught as an inviolable rule. Sometimes beginning a sentence with a conjunction gives prose just the right rhythm to create that highly desired conversational tone.

Correctness

Poor grammar and words used incorrectly make both the writer and the organization appear ignorant and sloppy. To hone your grammatical skills, work with a grammar guide next to you. (The use of writing tools is discussed later in this chapter.) Consult the guide when you are unsure about any writing issue. Make use of your word processor's grammar and spell check, but do not rely on them solely. Another way to work on grammar issues is to create a *never again* table (see Table 1.3). This is a three-column table (see the following sample) that lists a grammatical error, the rule that governs the problem, and a mnemonic device to remember the solution. When you keep a list of grammatical errors and refer to it as you compose, you will eventually learn to correct the problem. Keep adding and erasing errors until you no longer need to consult the chart.

TABLE 1.3 Never again table

Grammar problem	Rule	Mnemonic device
Its versus It's	It's **always** = it is	The dog bites its tail because it's plagued with fleas.
Effect versus affect	Effect = noun Affect = verb	Ibuprofen adversely affects my stomach, but the medicine's effect cures my headache.

Parallelism

Good writing often uses a device called parallelism, or parallel structure. Writers use parallelism instinctually because it appeals to our natural desire for symmetry. Parallelism matches nouns with nouns, verbs with verbs, and phrases with phrases: "For *faster* action, *less* stomach upset, and *more* for your money, use XX." Readers expect parallelism, especially in sets of two or three items, and in bulleted and enumerated lists. Using parallel phrasing correctly is key to writing in the workplace.

Positive Voice

Positive voice uses affirmative words to make a point. For example, instead of saying, "We are out of green T-shirts," we would emphasize the positive and say, "Order any size of our orange and gray T-shirts." Avoid downbeat words or words than can convey a negative connotation and rephrase in a positive way. Instead of, "No coupons will be honored after April 30," say, "Coupons will be honored through April 30."

Reliance on Strong Nouns and Verbs

Good writing uses nouns and verbs to do the heavy work and saves adverbs and adjectives for rare occasions. Instead of "Our brightly-colored, twinkling lights will be reminders of the happiest, most memorable times you and your family will ever enjoy," say, "Our dazzling lights will twinkle their way into your family's memories." Replace "Our auto policies are competitive," with "Our auto policies beat the competition's." Avoid using the most boring and overused verb in the English language: to be. Check for overuse of *is*, *are*, *were*, and *was* and see if you can eliminate them by using a stronger, more specific verb. We can't entirely avoid adverbs or adjectives or *to be*, but we can be mindful of how often we use them.

Sentence Variety

Sentence variety is linked to conversational prose and has two elements. The first is sentence beginnings.

As you edit, look at the way your sentences begin. Do three in a row begin with *The*? Do two sentences within two paragraphs begin with *There are*? Avoid writing sentences that begin with the same word or phrase. The second way to attain sentence variety is to vary sentence length. Short, choppy sentences make prose annoyingly staccato. Natural-sounding prose combines short, medium, and longer sentences.

One way to check your sentence length is to look at how the periods line up. If you see a vertical or slanted line of periods, you need to alter some of the sentence lengths. This can be accomplished in several ways. Join two sentences whose content is closely linked by embedding the gist of one sentence into another. Combine two sentences with a coordinate conjunction to create a complex sentence. Or try an alternate sentence beginning such as an introductory phrase, which will add sentence variety.

Simple Words

Avoid jargon. Always, always, always choose the simpler, more recognizable word over the longer, more showy one. Instead of *rhinovirus* say *a cold*. Opt for *e-mail* over *electronic message*. In *utilize* versus *use*, *use* wins! (Also notice how the number of words your reader has to wade through goes down with simpler words.)

Shorter Paragraphs

Long paragraphs are appropriate for essays, but they have no place in professional documents. Big blocks of type scare readers away. The longest paragraph should be no more than six to eight lines. Always be aware of how a paragraph appears on a page (or a screen) and take pity on your audience—don't make your reader slog through dense prose.

Style: Formal versus Informal

Writers must wear different hats and adjust their writing style—sometimes called voice or tone—to the task at hand. In professional writing, we always aim for a natu-

TABLE 1.4 Formal and informal writing styles

	Formal style	Informal style
Types of documents	Letters Long reports Research Proposals	Most communication within the organization including e-mail, IM, memos, text messages Routine messages to outside audiences Informal reports
Characteristics	No personal pronouns (I, we) No contractions Objective voice or use of passive voice No figurative language or clichés No editorializing Limited use of adjectives No exclamation points Longer sentences Some technical language	Use of personal pronouns Use of contractions Shorter sentences, easily recognizable words Limited use of warm, inoffensive humor

ral style, as mentioned earlier. However, we must sometimes be even more specific about the style we choose.

Choosing to use an informal or formal writing style depends on the audience and the document's purpose. There is no clear-cut way to determine when to use each style; sometimes, an e-mail may require formality. Most of the time, however, e-mails are informal. To determine which style fits your needs, understand that informal writing allows the writer and reader to connect on a more personal level. It can convey warmth. Formal writing, on the other hand, produces the impression of objectivity and professionalism.

Some genres, however, have generally accepted styles. Use Table 1.4 to help guide you in choosing which style best suits your task.

Writing Tools

Just as a doctor wouldn't enter an examination room without a stethoscope or a carpenter wouldn't pull up to a job site without a hammer, no writer can be without the tools of the trade: a good dictionary, thesaurus, and style guide.

Many excellent writing reference books are on the market, both in electronic and print format. I use both. Although I often visit www.dictionary.com when I compose, I also rely on my hard copy dictionary. Dictionaries in book format allow us to browse, and sometimes the writer will happen upon a word or meaning, which doesn't happen when you use Dictionary.com. The same goes for the thesaurus. I find the thesaurus built into Microsoft Word to be very weak. As a writer, I need to make the most out of the bounteous English language. A hard cover thesaurus is worth its weight in gold as far as I'm concerned. I use *Roget's 21st Century Thesaurus* edited by Barbara Ann Kipfer, PhD. I particularly like that it's organized like a dictionary.

Many good style guides are likewise available. For a grammar guide, I use Diana Hacker's *A Writer's Reference*, 7th edition, but many excellent grammar reference books are available.

Many good grammar websites can also be useful. The Grammar Book (http://www.grammarbook.com/) and the Purdue Online Writing Lab (https://owl.english.purdue.edu/) are handy and reliable websites to look up any grammar issues you may have.

The important thing to remember is to keep your tools nearby as you compose. The more you use these references, the less you'll need them. You will internalize the rules of writing as you use them.

Conclusion

Writing well on the job is key to career success. By breaking down writing into stages called the writing process, your end product is more likely to accomplish its ultimate purpose. When composing on the job, effective writers integrate many elements that will distinguish their work as professional, well-edited, and clear. Whether you choose hard copy or digital, use writing tools including a dictionary, thesaurus, and grammar guide to create professional documents. Doing so will help you excel in the workplace.

Avoiding Wordiness Checklist

Wordy phrase and example	Solution	✓
Avoid beginning a sentence with *There are* or *It is*. *There are four points that should be considered.* *It is clear that cashmere is warmer.*	Begin sentences with the true subject. *Consider these four points* or *Four points should be considered.* *Cashmere is clearly warmer.*	
Avoid beginning sentences with *That* or *This*. *Choosing teams should be done carefully. This is because a good mix will generate better results.*	Connect to previous sentence. *Choosing teams should be done carefully because a good mix will generate better results.*	
Use *active voice* rather than passive. *Rain forests are being destroyed by uncontrolled logging.*	Passive voice depletes prose of vitality and can almost always be rewritten in active voice. *Uncontrolled logging is destroying rain forests.*	
Omit *that* or *which* whenever possible. *The water heater that you install will last 15–20 years.*	Unless that or which is required for clarity, omit it. *The water heater you install will last 15–20 years.*	
Avoid prepositional phrase modifiers. *The committee of financial leaders meets every Tuesday.*	Replace with one-word modifiers. *The financial leaders committee meets every Tuesday.*	
Avoid *be* verbs. *New Orleans is one of the most vibrant cities in the United States.*	Replace with a strong verb. *New Orleans vibrates with activity like no other U.S. city.*	
Tighten closely related sentences of explanation. *When hanging wallpaper, three factors need to be considered. The factors are X, X, and X.*	Join closely related sentences of explanation with a colon to avoid repetitions. *When hanging wallpaper, consider three factors: X, X, and X.*	
Tighten closely related sentences. *MRIs are used to diagnose many ailments. MRIs create an image of organs and soft tissues to diagnose.*	Omit repetitious phrasing in second sentence. *MRIs diagnose many ailments by creating images of organs and soft tissues.*	
Tighten verb phrases with auxiliary + ing verbs *Management was holding a staff meeting.*	Replace is/are/was/were/have + verb with a one-word verb. *Management held a staff meeting.*	
Avoid using *there is/are* within a sentence. *When creating a mail list, there are many pitfalls.*	Find an active verb to replace *there is/are*. *When creating a mail list, many pitfalls exist.*	
Remove redundancies. *An anonymous stranger may be dangerous.*	Know the true meaning of a word. *Strangers may be dangerous.*	

Editing and Proofreading Checklist

Check your draft for the following	✓
Document content is tailored to meet the needs of the audience and attains writing purpose	
Copy is edited for conciseness	
Body paragraphs have unity and cohesion and are shortened for visual appeal	
Transitions in and between paragraphs adequately link ideas	
Grammar is correct	
Punctuation is used correctly	
Copy has good rhythm and flow; uses a natural and conversational tone	
Sentences show variety in beginning and length	
Names are spelled correctly; phone numbers and URLs are accurate	
Words are used correctly	
Capitalization is consistent and adheres to specific stylebook guidelines	
Document adheres to specific genre formatting guidelines	
Document shows professionalism	

Applying This Skill: Conciseness and Clarity

Revise the following sentences to improve the conciseness and clarity.

1. One thing that can be said to have greatly improved the presentation was the extra week of rehearsal.

2. The office manager was good at organizing. She also managed the schedule good and helped people with a friendly smile.

3. There are many executives who have not made any progress about the art of writing.

4. There is one supervisor who is of the opinion that this policy will prove destructive to the morale of employees.

5. The thing that prevented the committee from meeting was the stormy weather.

6. The snow was falling in such a way as to cover up the level parking lot, until soon nothing was visible to our eyes except for a thick blanket of dense snowfall.

7. This particular article is about things that can be done to help you along the way with salary negotiations.

_____
_____
_____
_____

8. As a result of the fact that he had never learned the basic fundamentals of grammar, he found writing difficult to such an extent that he had to withdraw from the course.

_____
_____
_____
_____

9. The following report touches on the process we took to complete our report along with an individual breakdown of each team member's contribution toward the project.

_____
_____
_____
_____

10. The supervisor was annoyed by the fact that we arrived late instead of on time.

_____
_____
_____
_____

11. It is recommended that all pages in the document be numbered correctly in the right order.

_____
_____
_____
_____

12. Attempts were made unsuccessfully by the division staff to assess the project.

_____
_____
_____
_____

Applying This Skill: Pronoun Use

Pronouns are words that replace nouns, such as he, she, it, they, and us. Using the correct pronouns ensures your writing is clear and understandable. Rewrite the following sentences to correct the pronoun errors.

1. The three most common devices are email, cell phone, and instant messages. They would all be lost without email.

   _____

   _____

   _____

   _____

2. I would like to transfer you to another branch location if they have internship openings.

   _____

   _____

   _____

   _____

3. When a member joins a gym, they discover the many benefits of exercise.

   _____

   _____

   _____

   _____

4. Our sales team will work with a client to ensure the products meet their needs.

   _____

   _____

   _____

   _____

5. The company is promoting their new product.

   _____

   _____

   _____

   _____

6. It is convenient to use text messaging to contact clients.

   _____

   _____

   _____

   _____

7. I tell students that when they are trying to save money, you should buy used textbooks.

   _____

   _____

   _____

Reading 5.4

Bad Writing Costs Businesses Billions

It's not just a chore to wade through the badly written memos, emails, and other lousy business communication—this inefficiency costs us insane amounts of money.

By Josh Bernoff

There is a fundamental inefficiency at the heart of American business. It is right in front of all of our faces, and yet we fail to recognize it.

It's the fuzzy, terrible writing we slog through every day at work. And it's costing American businesses nearly $400 billion every year.

Think about it. You start your day wading through first-draft emails from colleagues who fail to come to the point. You consume reports that don't make clear what's happening or what your management should do about it. The websites, marketing materials, and press releases from your suppliers are filled with jargon and meaningless superlatives. This problem is as common as rust, and just as welcome; in my survey of business-people who write at work, 81 percent agreed with the statement: "Poorly written material wastes a lot of my time."

Poor writing creates a drag on everything you do. It functions like a tax, sapping your profits, and I can quantify it. American workers spend 22 percent of their work time reading; higher compensated workers read more. According to my analysis, America is spending 6 percent of total wages on time wasted attempting to get meaning out of poorly written material. Every company, every manager, every professional pays this tax, which consumes $396 billion of our national income. That's more than half of what we pay for Medicare—but the poor writing tax pays for nothing but waste.

We're so immersed in this stuff that we hardly notice it any more. I'm talking about job descriptions like this one, from a health care company:

> "The Area Vice President, Enterprise Customers will develop and manage a sustainable strategic relationship that transforms the current commercial model by creating joint value that results in the ongoing reduction of costs, continuous process improvement, growth and profitability for both partners with the ability to export key learnings."

How much time did the HR department and the job candidates waste trying to figure that out?

How about the lede from ++ Samsung's recent statement ++ about its smartphones?

[https://news.samsung.com/global/statement-on-galaxy-note7]

> "Samsung is committed to producing the highest quality products and we take every incident report from our valued customers very seriously. In response to recently reported cases of the new Galaxy Note7, we conducted a thorough investigation and found a battery cell issue."

Battery cell issue? The phones are catching on fire—but you'd never know it from the company's statement, which mentions only "incidents." *Say what you mean.*

Of all the serious problems in the American workplace, this one is the most solvable. And we can solve it one company, one culture, one worker at a time.

The first step is to adopt what I call "The Iron Imperative" in everything you write: *treat the reader's time as more valuable than your own.* To embrace it means that every time you send an email or write a document, you must take a moment to structure it for maximum readability and meaning. We are lazy; we'd rather save our own time than someone else's. But writers who adopt The Iron Imperative stand out in the workplace for clarity and efficiency, and are more likely to get ahead. Workplace cultures that adopt it will reduce their poor writing tax.

Recognize that everybody reads on a screen now—either a smartphone or a computer screen. That reduces attention spans and concentration, which in turn demands a radical rethink of the way you communicate in writing. In this environment, brevity must become a core value. Regardless of what you write, the title or subject line and the first two sentences must carry the payload. Unlike Samsung in its press release, you must never bury the lede.

People use jargon to impress other people—but for each person you impress, many others are just confused. Clear, plain language communicates better, is easier to consume, and is more likely to get its point across to more people.

A primary cause of incoherent writing is committeespeak—documents that become a pastiche of contradictory comments inserted based on management reviewers. In my survey, only 32 percent of writers thought that their process for collecting and combining feedback worked well. Along with clarity, brevity, and plain language, a disciplined and coherent review process goes a long way toward improving the quality of the documents we're struggling to get meaning from.

It's not that hard to embrace clear, pointed, and direct writing that doesn't waste the reader's time. Commit to do that, and to eliminate the poor writing tax at your company. You'll get ahead. And you'll make American business a little more efficient while you're at it.

Applying This Skill: Parallelism

Rewrite the following sentences to make them parallel.

1. At my last job, I:

   - Participate in meetings
   - Strengthened interpersonal skills
   - Lead and participated in teams

   _____

   _____

   _____

   _____

2. We all want to find happiness by reducing stress, positive habits, and to be a healthy weight.

   _____

   _____

   _____

   _____

3. The job requires applicants:

   - Basic knowledge of marketing
   - Knowledge of different cultures
   - Completed international business courses
   - Speaking, reading, and listening fluently in Spanish and English

   _____

   _____

   _____

   _____

4. If you want to succeed in this course, you must listen carefully, read the material, attend class, and be participating.

   _____

   _____

   _____

   _____

5. The company must either increase sales or it will be necessary to reduce expenses.

   _____

   _____

   _____

   _____

Applying This Skill: Numbers

Rewrite the following sentences correctly using numbers.

1. 2013 was a very productive year for the company.

_____

_____

_____

_____

2. We sold eight units this week but were aiming to sell 11 by the 1st of the month.

_____

_____

_____

_____

3. The meeting is scheduled for December 1st, but we need to change it to December 10th.

_____

_____

_____

_____

4. Please review the company's two new client files by October 15th.

_____

_____

_____

_____

5. By September 1st, 2014, the website should be live.

_____

_____

_____

_____

6. The last outbreak of smallpox occurred in the late seventy's.

_____

_____

_____

_____

7. Can you meet for lunch at 12:00 noon?

_____

_____

_____

_____

Applying This Skill: Active and Passive Verbs

Active verb sentences clearly identify who is doing an action in a sentence. In *passive verb* sentences, who or what does the action of the sentence is implied, unknown, or comes after the verb in the sentence. Passive verbs are often used when a writer wants to deflect blame or criticism or when the action of the sentence is more important than the doer/actor.

Confused? Consider these examples:

- The report was requested.
- My boss requested the report.

Which sentence has the passive verb? The first sentence's verb ("was requested") is passive. The sentence does not identify *who* requested the report. The second sentence clearly states who did the action—the requesting—which leaves no room for confusion or conjecture.

For most people, determining whether a verb is active or passive is very difficult at first. The easiest way to determine if a verb is active or passive is to ask the following:

- What is the verb (the action word)?
- Who/what is doing the action (verb)?
    - If you know who is acting = active verb
    - If you're unsure who is acting = passive verb

Here is how to use these questions to identify active and passive verbs.

The sentence is: Companies expect accounting positions to increase in the next ten years.

1. What is the verb? Expect
2. Who/what is expecting? Companies
3. The actor is clearly named before the verb, so this sentence is *active*.

The sentence is: The report was left on the desk.

1. What is the verb? Left or was left
2. Who/what left the report? We don't know.
3. Who performed the action in this sentence is unknown; therefore, this sentence is *passive*.
4. Fixed: Susie left the report on the desk.

The sentence is: Several students were failed because of poor writing.

1. What is the verb? Failed, were failed
2. Who failed the students? We don't know. Did the professor fail the students? Did the assessment team fail the students? This sentence is *passive*.
3. Fixed: The professor failed several students because of poor writing.

Sometimes, a sentence includes who or what did the action of the verb, but it is *after* the verb, which generally makes for wordy sentences.

For example: Several students were failed by the department because of poor writing.

1. What is the verb? Failed, were failed
2. Who failed the students? The department did. We know who did the action, but it appears *after* the verb. This sentence is *passive*.
3. Fixed: The department failed several students because of poor writing.

Identify whether the sentences below have an active or a passive verb. Rewrite the sentence using the opposite verb form.

1. The interview was conducted by Jane, who is the recruiter at the company.

   _____
   _____
   _____

2. I assigned each team member a different task.

   _____
   _____
   _____

3. All of our employees are encouraged to read the employee handbook to understand the company's expectations.

   _____
   _____
   _____

4. You may add more detail to your resume to make it stronger.

   _____
   _____
   _____

5. People from other cultures can offer insights Americans may not have considered.

   _____
   _____
   _____

6. A dress code needs to be established for this company.

   _____
   _____
   _____

7. I'm sorry I cannot fulfill your request.

   _____
   _____
   _____

Applying This Skill: Word Choice

Rewrite the following sentences using different word choice.

Consideration is one of the 5 Cs of communication that relates to the tone and choice of words an author uses.

Positive vs. Negative Wording

Negative: We cannot process your order because your payment information is not correct.

Positive: _____

_____

Negative: We do not answer phone calls after 3 p.m. on Fridays.

Positive: _____

_____

Writer Centered (You) vs. Reader Centered

Writer: We shipped the order this morning with a 3–5-day delivery.

Reader: _____

_____

Writer: We are pleased to award you scholarship.

Reader: _____

_____

General vs. Specific

General: The class was good.

Specific: _____

_____

General: Please complete the forms as soon as possible.

Specific: _____

_____

Gender Biased vs. Gender Neutral

Biased: Each person must complete his homework on time.

Neutral: _____

_____

Biased: Foreman

Neutral: _____

_____

Biased: The best man for the job.

Neutral: _____

_____

Clichés vs. Direct/Clear

Cliché: Don't throw the baby out with the bathwater.

Direct: _____

_____

Cliché: It's all black and white.

Direct: _____

_____

Old-Fashioned Wording vs. Clear Phrasing

Outdated: As per your request, please find the enclosed form.

Clear: _____

_____

Outdated: I refer to your application of the 24th last month regarding your suitability for the post of sales clerk.

Clear: _____

_____

Formal vs. Informal

Formal: terminate   utilize   remunerate   appeal

Informal: _____

_____

Applying This Skill: Word Choice 2

Revise the following sentence to remove wordiness, to use the correct form of who/that, and to improve word choice.

1. I don't have any contacts that are in my field of study.
   _____
   _____
   _____
   _____

2. I would like to land an internship this spring.
   _____
   _____
   _____
   _____

3. Down the road, I see myself in a management position.
   _____
   _____
   _____
   _____

4. I am fairly strong when it comes to oral communication and I feel like my job really helps a lot with that because I use it every time I am talking to customers.
   _____
   _____
   _____
   _____

5. One business professional in my field that could be interviewed is James Joe, my manager.
   _____
   _____
   _____
   _____

6. I am a nontraditional student that has recently returned to college after taking a break.
   _____
   _____
   _____
   _____

7. It is strong verbal skills that I have developed by explaining a process or concept to a person and by talking them through it.
   _____
   _____
   _____
   _____

8. I intend to begin looking for references that can assist me in my job search.

    _____
    _____
    _____
    _____

9. The reason why I chose to interview this person is because she is my manager.

    _____
    _____
    _____
    _____

10. The money was used to pay off student loans deemed uncollectable by the banks who funded them.

    _____
    _____
    _____
    _____

Summing Up Unit I: Foundations

After completing the lessons in Unit I, you have a good foundation on which to build your skills throughout the course. After completing Unit I, you should be able to:

- Understand how to properly introduce yourself and someone else
- Identify and apply the 5Cs of Communication
- Deliver constructive feedback
- Use the editing and revising process
- Demonstrate the ability to write concisely and clearly
- Apply a variety to stylistic writing elements effectively (vocabulary, pronouns, parallelism etc.)

You may want to review the 5Cs of Communication and various writing activities as the course progresses because they will continue to be the foundations for effective communication.

Formats

- ► Business Letters and Memos
- ► Email
- ► Bad-News Messages
- ► Business Meetings
- ► Internet and Social Media

Written Business Communication Formats

Business communications have very specific formats and types; it is important for you to know and use these formats effectively. Following formatting conventions indicates your knowledge of the standards, attention to detail, and desire to present you and your company in the best possible way. Some companies will have specific style guidelines to follow; when such guidance doesn't exist, you should follow the standard formats you learn here.

In Part Two, you will learn about different written formats (letter, memo, email) and when to use them, business meetings, and writing for the web and social media. The chart below briefly describes and compares the various types of business communication.

The most common types of business communication are:
- Letters
- Memos
- Emails
- Meetings
- Web and social media

Document Medium Comparison

Characteristic	Letter	Memo	Email	Online	Social Media
Audience	External	Internal	External or Internal	External or Internal	External or Internal
Use of visual enhancements (bold, italics, subheads, bullets etc.)	✓	✓	✓	✓	✓
Tone	Formal	Impersonal	Friendly Professional	Friendly Professional	Informal Professional
Single Spacing, with blank line between paragraphs	✓	✓	✓	✓	✓
Salutation & Closing	Yes, formal	No	Yes, less formal	Based on Situation	Based on Situation
Signature	✓				
Short paragraphs	✓	✓	✓	✓	✓
Sections with descriptive subheads	✓	✓	✓	✓	✓

FIGURE 6.1 Infographic: Document Medium Comparison

6   Letters and Memos

Two common business communications are letters and memos. Letters are the most formal of business communications. Letters are typically meant for an external audience (i.e., someone outside of the company, such as clients, customers, or business partners). Memos are very different: they are internal documents, meant for employees and departments. The following readings will describe letters and memos in more detail. After completing this lesson, you will:

- Know when to use a business letter or business memo
- Know and demonstrate use of business letter format
- Know and demonstrate use of business memo format

Reading 6.1

Write Effective Letters and Memos

By Everett Chasen and Bob Putnam

"If I had more time, I would have written a shorter letter."

—T.S. Eliot

The Parts of a Letter

Many large organizations have correspondence guides that describe how people should write letters on company stationery. Even if you work in one of those organizations, there are likely to be times when you can't consult the manual. And if you don't work for an organization that has a manual, you'll need some help. For your ready reference, here are pointers for how a letter should be organized.

At the very top of the letter is the *letterhead*, which identifies your company and provides the address where any return correspondence should be sent.

Right beneath the address at the left margin, put the *date* on which you've written the letter or the date you intend for it to be mailed—whichever is later. You'd be amazed at how important the date is—people file your letter using it; it's a great way to avoid confusion in responses ("In your April 23 letter, you said ..."); and it's a reminder to your correspondent that her reply is timely or not—so please, do not omit the date.

Some people add a reference line below the date, which is useful when you're writing to a large company

and don't know to whom to send your letter, or if you're answering a specific letter. This is also a good place for reference numbers, such as a case number or purchase order number.

Next comes the *name and address* of the person to whom you are writing. In many large offices, most mail is opened by someone other than the addressee, and sometimes the envelope gets lost in the transfer—which is why you have to put the name and address inside, too, to make sure the letter gets where it's supposed to go.

After that comes the *salutation*, or greeting, a traditional ritual followed by letter writers for hundreds of years. In business letters, the salutation almost always begins with "Dear," and is followed by either "Ms. Smith," or "John" or "Sir or Madam" or some variation on one of those themes. Follow the salutation with a colon—not a comma.

Some people include a *subject line* to follow the salutation (don't bother if you've already inserted a reference line below the date.) Emails, which almost always have subjects, have influenced letters because in the past letters did not have subject lines. Subject lines help your reader know, at a glance, what your letter's about. If you use one, keep it short. Finally, you get to the body of the letter. We'll discuss this in more detail below.

After the *body* of text, end your letter with a closing. This is a phrase like "Sincerely," or "Very truly yours," or "Best regards." If your organization doesn't specify the phrase to use in your closing, pick something that reflects the tone of your letter, as long as it's respectful.

Leave five blank lines after that and type in your name. As a manager, you should put your title and your company name on lines under your name. Of course, the blank space is for you to sign your name—so that whoever gets the letter knows you've at least seen it, even if you ascend far enough up the ranks that someone else writes your letters for you.

The Body of a Business Letter

Even if you skipped over the previous section because your current company has a style manual that determines what all letters will look like, here's the part you should not skip—unless you want to write lots more cover letters before your next promotion. What makes a good business letter? It's a letter that:

- **Is brief:** People don't have time to read long letters anymore. Ask yourself the question: "What do I want my audience to do or to know after reading this letter?" Then answer that question as close to the beginning of the letter as possible.
- **Is warm and friendly, not cold and impersonal:** Part of the goal of most business letters is not only to convey information, but also to build a business relationship. A letter filled with legalisms, fancy words, or Latin phrases will not be perceived as an example of your extraordinary intellect or vocabulary. It will only appear pretentious and wordy. The KISS acronym "keep it short and simple," originated in the design community, but it applies here.
- **Is written at an appropriate level of familiarity:** In making the letter friendly, you have to consider your audience. The person you write to also plays an important part in determining the tone of your letter. You can be more familiar, of course, with someone you know than with a stranger, but you must also write differently to your boss than to your colleagues or to anyone who reports to you.
- **Is organized in a logical manner:** In every good letter—in fact every good written document—sentence follows sentence in a logical way, just as B follows A. Don't jump around between topics. If you introduce more than one concept, make sure you've completed your discussion of the first topic before you move on to the second.
- **Is persuasive:** In most cases, you will ask your readers to take some action after they read what you have to say. You need to persuade or educate them to take the action you want. Provide them with the information they need to agree with you, presented in a logical and factual manner.
- **Emphasizes the positive:** Avoid using negative words such as can't, won't, and impossible. Instead, a good letter emphasizes what you can do. Instead of "We no longer make those widgets," try "Although our popular widget model A-123 is sold out, we have a new model A-124 that may fit your needs. I've enclosed a product brochure that describes its features."
- **Uses the writing skills described in chapter 3:** Always write using active voice, not passive; keep your words short; cut whatever you can; avoid jargon and foreign phrases; and above all, be courteous. Even if you're writing a complaint letter, or responding to an angry customer who, in your opinion, is way off base—keep your cool. You can, indeed, catch more flies with honey than with vinegar, and even if your objective in writing is something other than catching flies, being civil in your correspondence is the right thing to do for your company and your own reputation.

Before starting to write, think of a one-sentence description of what you hope to accomplish through your words. Use that description to create your first draft—and then pare down the draft to what is essential. Don't put that description in your letter. Review your logic, check vocabulary for readability and negativity, proofread carefully, confirm the gender of your recipient, and send it out. Of course, if others draft letters for your review or signature, it's doubly important you look for all these things before giving your approval, since your staff may not have the same point of view as yours. You may have to send many letters back for a while, marked up with your corrections, but eventually your staff will figure out what you're looking for.

A Sample Business Letter

The Balmy Lip Balm Company
123 Sunny Day Lane
Key West, FL 33040

Ms. Angelina Jolie
The Mansion On The Hill
Beverly Hills, CA 90210

Subject: Our new lip balm product

Dear Ms. Jolie:

Thank you for your letter praising our company's former lip balm product. The reason you can no longer find the old version of Balmy's Lip Balm in Beverly Hills, California is because we are in the process of replacing it with a newer version we are confident you will appreciate and enjoy.

The rumor you have heard is true: We will be replacing the secret ingredient in our formula. This is because bats are becoming an endangered species, and it was increasingly difficult to obtain sufficient quantities of the bat waste by-product we were using. (Of course, we would never harm any actual bats!)

I hope you will agree that our new synthetic formula lip balm, which uses no human or animal product or waste material, will be as good as, if not better than, our previous product. I am enclosing a free sample of the new Balmy's Lip Balm, so you can see for yourself just how good it is. I am sure the career successes you attribute to our old lip balm will continue once you've tried our new one.

Thank you for being such a good customer in the past, and enjoy the sample!

Sincerely,

I.M. Balmy
President, Balmy Lip Balm

FIGURE 6.2

Writing Memos

Writing coaches and college business courses focus most on letter writing, but it is the humble memo, or memorandum, that still makes the business world go around. Memos can be addressed to a group of people. Even when they are addressed to one person, there will be other readers. A well-written memo can make or break a career. It actually did for one of us. As a brand new government employee, Ev wrote a memo on the operating hours of a lock and dam in Troy, New York, and got noticed by senior leadership as someone who could make a coherent argument in writing.

Expert Tip

As the director of executive correspondence for a large government agency, **Katrice Pasteur** and her staff of 12 review between 5–10,000 letters, memos, and reports every year. "Letters are still extremely important in business," she says. According to Katrice, a good letter:

- **Addresses all of the correspondent's concerns, without dancing around the issues.** "Get to the bottom-line issues in the beginning—and make sure the writer doesn't have to write back again and tell you that you didn't answer his question."

- **Doesn't beat around the bush.** If the answer is no, it's no. "And don't try to overwhelm your correspondence with information they didn't ask for, either—that just invites them to write back again and ask more questions."

- **Is consistent with other correspondence you've written.** "It's OK to say the same thing to different people."

Typically, memos are to the point. Most memos do one of four things: they provide information or directions to their readers; they record agreements between groups (these are often called "memorandums of agreement" or "memorandums of understanding"); they allow an action to take place; or they make an argument in favor of, or opposed to, a course of action. To maintain clarity and directness, you should limit the number of points you make in a memo. If you have several points to make, you should separate them into more than one memo, or call for a meeting.

Because memos are usually internal documents, they are more informal than letters but are more formal than emails. Also, because they are internal, most organizations have templates for preparing them. If you're managing a small business, however, and develop your own forms and procedures, Microsoft Word has several memo templates you can use. They include a:

To: line, in which you enter the name of the memo's principal audience, or the group or organization it is being sent to.

From: line, in which you enter your name, your title, or both.

Date: line, in which you enter the date (but you knew that, didn't you)?

Subject: or **Re:** (for reference) line, in which you explain the subject of your memo. Take time to write a subject that will get the attention of your reader, while still being appropriate. With all the emails today's business executive receives, and all the letters and other information they read, your memo needs to stand out. So make sure the subject line interests them.

The body of the memo follows the subject line. What you put in the body depends on your purpose for writing the memo.

- If you're *providing information* to your readers, it's usually to help them make a decision. Give them good, solid information, simply presented. As a manager, it's your job to present not only the good news, but also the bad. Don't bury the truth under an avalanche of words. Remember the letter will be a permanent record. Try to anticipate what your readers already know. It's no use to anyone to go into detail about general, easy issues. If you do, they won't read what's really important.

- If you're *recording an agreement*, be comprehensive. Make sure to include all the pertinent details. In the future, it will be an important record, and will be used when there are questions about what each party in the agreement actually meant.

- If you're *allowing something to take place*, be especially brief. "Effective June 1, Jane Jones will be acting director of our Marketing Division," tells readers all they need to know (unless, of course, you want to add a brief biography of Jane to introduce her).

- If you're *making an argument,* which is the most difficult form of memo writing, keep your writing simple, so your argument is understood. Summarize your argument in the first paragraph—not the last—so readers understand right away what you're thinking and can follow your thoughts

---

A Sample Memorandum

To: All Organization Members

From: Avon Barksdale, Chief Executive

Date: August 15, 2012

Subject: Appointment of Stringer Bell as Acting Chief Executive

As many of you know, I have recently been called out of town on a special assignment. While I am endeavoring to return to headquarters as quickly as possible, and will remain in touch with the organization via phone, email, and occasional face-to-face meetings, I believe it is necessary to appoint someone to manage the day-to-day aspects of our organization while I am away.

Accordingly, I have asked Russell 'Stringer' Bell to assume the role as Acting Chief Executive during the period of my absence. Stringer has been my right-hand man in the past, and is fully familiar with all aspects of our operation. In addition, he and I will consult on a regular basis, so you may assume that any direction he provides has my full approval.

I hope you will provide Stringer with the same level of cooperation and loyalty you have provided me in the past. As I have only a limited capability to receive phone calls and emails on my current assignment, please contact him directly if you have any questions regarding this memo, or any other subject.

Thank you for your continued support,

Avon Barksdale

FIGURE 6.3

---

clearly. Make transitions from one step of your argument to the next; order your thoughts in a logical manner (using topic headings can help you do that); and write a conclusion that sums up everything you said and what you want readers to do.

Many people use numbers or bulleted lists to make the information they present easily accessible. Whether you use these or not, you should write short, concise paragraphs. The usual writing rules apply for any memo, especially about using active voice, using easy-to-follow vocabulary, and being civil. In memos about assigning responsibility, make sure it's clear to whom those responsibilities have been assigned.

For many years, it was commonly accepted practice in memos to close without a signature or a closing other than "For additional information, please contact…" Nowadays, many people sign off on their memos, either with a signature above their typed name or with a close like "Sincerely." Remember that in a memo, your title is in the From: line, so it's different from letter writing, where your title is at the bottom with your typed name and signature. It is a good new trend to sign memos.

As a manager, you should read all the memos you receive carefully—not only for their content, but also to help you conform memos you write to the organization's accepted style. And keep this last rule in mind: If you're writing to an outside organization, use a letter; if it's within the organization, write a memo; and if your memo is more than two pages long, consider a report instead.

Reading 6.2

Basics of Document Design

By Janet Mizrahi

One of the most important elements of workplace writing is a document's appearance. Writing in professional contexts requires as much attention to the way a document appears on the page or the screen as its content. The reason is that as writers, we must make the task of reading easy for our audience. If you have ever waded through dense pages of text with long paragraphs or tried to follow a single line of type that goes across an 18-inch computer screen, you know that reading can become tedious if good design is not factored into what your eyes must look at.

In this chapter, we'll cover the basics of document design for print and screen. We will discuss the conventions of document design as they pertain to specific genres in the remaining chapters.

Print Document Design

Writing for a printed page differs from writing for a screen not just in the words we write but in the way the words look on the page. This is called **page layout.** You are probably aware of certain elements of page layout without knowing it. For example, use of columns and choice of landscape or portrait view are part of page layout.

When composing a document that will be printed, first consider page size. Is your document for standard sized paper (8.5 × 11 in.) or smaller? If you are creating a trifold brochure, for example, you will be laying out the words very differently than if you are writing a report. In both cases, however, consider the z pattern. The z pattern (see Figure 6.4) is the way readers of English approach a page. Our eye begins at the top left of the page and scans to the right, going back and forth, left to right, until we reach the bottom. This pattern is significant because words or images that fall along the z hold the eye's attention more than the areas surrounding the z. Savvy writers will put words and images they want the reader to focus on along this path.

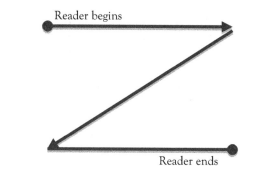

FIGURE 6.4 z pattern of reading.

Elements of Page Layout

Each page contains design elements you will want to consider as follows.

Color

Although black is always the preferred color for body type, some color can add visual interest to print pages. Color can be used for document headings, in charts and graphs, or as ways to highlight information. Avoid using bright colors for type and understand that the way a color appears on the screen will likely differ from its reproduction on the printed page. Also remember that you will need a color printer for your color scheme to show!

Graphical Elements

Adding graphical elements to your documents such as boldface, bullets, enumeration, italics, or underlining serve varied functions. **Boldface** calls attention to words and phrases. It is commonly used for headings and sparingly used to highlight words or phrases. **Bulleted points** are used to list items and to attract the reader's eye. Bulleted points break up text, too. **Enumeration** (listing items 1., 2., 3., etc.) is used to indicate a series in order. *Italics* are used for emphasis, to indicate a word in a different language, for proper names, and for titles. **Underlining** can indicate a title or emphasis.

A quick word on the use of CAPS. Beware that the reader will interpret type in all caps as a scream. The only time I use all caps is in a context in which I must conform to a text-only design. In that case, I use caps for headings. I never use all caps and boldface, however. It is not only redundant but also truly a signal for translating the words into a scream.

No graphical elements should be overused, and writers should avoid including too many on any one page. Doing so clutters the page and ends up having the opposite effect from what was intended.

Headings and Subheadings

Headings name categories of information. They summarize the content that follows and are organized by levels: first level heading, second level heading, and so forth. Headings can be viewed as the points of an outline, and their use is a primary way writers organize content. For the reader, headings serve as graphic markers that signal a new topic. They help the reader easily focus on specific areas of interest. Headings break up text, making material more visually attractive and easier on the eye.

Subheadings are mini-headings, or subsections of a heading. They, too, break up long text and enhance visual appeal.

In a print document, headings are indicated by use of a graphical device such as centering, boldface, or caps. Headings often use a contrasting type font. For example, if the body of a report were Times New Roman, you might want to use Arial for headings.

Header and Footer

Using a header and footer is a way to unify a document. Headers and footers also provide a location of page numbers or add graphic design features such as a company logo.

Margins

Most business documents have page margins all around of 1 to 1.5 in. Page margins are important because they create white space to make a page look uncluttered. Another aspect of margins is **justification**. Word processing programs give you four options for your margins: left justified with a ragged right edge, centered, right justified with ragged left, and fully justified. Table 6.1 illustrates the types of margin justification and when each should be used.

TABLE 6.1 Type justification

Type justification	Functionality
This margin is left justified, ragged right type. This margin is left justified, ragged right. This margin is left justified, ragged right.	Notice how the left margin forms a straight line, while the right edge is jagged. This is considered the easiest alignment to read and should be used in nearly every writing situation.
This is centered type. This is centered type. This is centered	Centered type is inappropriate for most reading tasks but is a good choice for headings, such as the headings in this table.
This is right justified type with a ragged left margin this is right justified type with a ragged left margin	Readers' eyes would quickly tire if having to readjust to locate the beginning of each line of type. Use right justified type to align short phrases only.
This line is considered fully justified. This line is considered fully justified. This line is considered fully justified. This line is considered fully justified.	Notice the awkward spaces between the words when using fully justified text. This occurs because the word processor does not hyphenate words so it has to create spaces to fit the type into a rectangle. Those spaces slow down reading. When full justification is needed for particular documents, you will need to use your own appropriate word hyphenations to reduce the space gaps that otherwise occur.

Paragraph Length

In college papers, it is not unusual for a paragraph to take up an entire typed page. However, that this is unacceptable in all business documents. To aid our readers, business writers limit paragraph length to no more than eight lines (not eight sentences.) This is a rule of thumb that should be taken very seriously. Long, dense paragraphs scare readers away.

Spacing

Again, in college, papers are usually double spaced and new paragraphs are indented. However, in business documents, single spacing is the norm; new paragraphs are signaled by adding an extra space. Because the extra space is clearly a marker of a new paragraph, it would be redundant and unnecessary to also use a tab.

Typeface

Type fonts are divided into two basic families: *serif* and *sans serif*. Serif fonts such as Times, Garamond, or Palatino have feet and tails under the letters that form a line to help the eye track the words and sentences, which is why graphic artists choose serif fonts for long documents such as books. Serif fonts have an old fashioned feel. For business documents that will be printed, using a serif font will help your reader move through the content faster.

Sans serif fonts like Helvetica, Arial, and Verdana have a cleaner, simple line that translates better to the pixel-based display on screens.

Look at the following example to examine the difference between font families:

This is 12-point Garamond, a serif font.

This is 12-point Arial, a sans serif font.

Notice the difference in the two 12-point fonts. Both are 12-point, but Arial appears much larger than Garamond. When you choose your font, you will want to take into consideration how large or small it appears on the page.

White Space

Space on a page without any visual or type is called white space. White space breaks up text and frames the words on the page. It also helps balance a page. It is helpful to view your page in the *preview* function of the word processing tool you use to see how the white space is arranged on the page. This is an excellent way to adjust pages that are off balance or too densely packed with words.

Notes

1   Nielsen (1996).
2   Nielsen, J. February 1, 1996. "In Defense of Print." Nielsonnormangroup.com. http://www.nngroup.com/articles/in-defense-of-print/ (accessed January 19, 2015).

Business Letter

Business letters are the most formal business communication. Your writing style and the formatting details (such as punctuation, salutation, and closing) contribute to the formality and demonstrate your understanding of business communication. A sample letter and checklist to use when editing your work appear below.

Assess Your Document Here   **Business Letter Format & Editing Checklist**

☐ ⟶ Sender's Address Here
Street Name
City, State, Zip Code

☐ ⟶ Date Here

☐ ⟶ Addressee's Name here
Address Here
City, State, Zip Code

☐ ⟶ Salutation Here:

☐ ⟶ Introduction Paragraph: Open with the main idea (deductive approach).
Include reason for writing and outline of information to follow in the
document (outline statement).

☐ ⟶ Body paragraph 1: Start with topic sentence. Include supporting information.
Use specific details and in-text citations when appropriate.

☐ ⟶ Body paragraph 2: Use basic body paragraph organization. Use visual
enhancements and design elements as needed, including bullets, bold,
italics, and subheadings. Remember and apply the Cs of Communication.

☐ ⟶ Body paragraph (if needed):

☐ ⟶ Conclusion: Provide a sense of closure. Remind reader of main point; include
action steps if needed. Include a forward-looking statement and include
contact statement (who reader should contact for more information).

☐ ⟶ Complementary Close,

☐ ⟶ Signature here

☐ ⟶ Sender's Name
Sender's Title, if appropriate

☐ ⟶ Enclosure Notation, if needed

FIGURE 6.5 Letter sample and checklist.

Applying This Skill: Identify Parts of Business Letter

Form student groups of 3–4 people. Your instructor will distribute envelopes containing parts of the business letter. Work to arrange the puzzle pieces into formal business letter format.

Assignment: Introduction Letter

Please write a business letter introducing yourself. The letter must be kept to one page and must follow the business letter format. The font size should be no less than 11 pt. and should be Times New Roman.

This assignment is designed to help me know more about you, your writing skills, and your ability to create professional-looking and -sounding documents.

Please address the letter to me, your professor.

Your introductory paragraph (3–4 sentences) should tell me a little about yourself. You can tell me a little about your family, where you were born, your high school activities/graduation date, any other postsecondary education, etc.

The body (2–4 short paragraphs) should address the following:

- **Education background.** Tell me about your major and how you chose that field (if you haven't selected a major, what direction do you think you might go), how many credit/courses you are taking this quarter, university participation/involvement, any study-abroad experiences and/or travels in other countries, any internship experiences or plans to intern prior to graduation, etc.
- **Work experiences/volunteer commitments.** Tell me about your current work situation: where, how many hours, major responsibilities, etc. Also, what job title would you like to have when you graduate, long-range job goals (after you've worked ten years), etc.? Where do you volunteer and why?
- **Communication experience.** Tell me about your strengths and weaknesses in the area of communication (written, oral, technological usage, etc.), types of communication you do on your job, what you expect to get out of this course, etc.

Your closing paragraph should provide a sense of closure. Mention any concerns, hopes, or expectations you have about the course. Please include the best way to contact you.

Memos

Memos are among the most common business documents, although they are frequently being replaced or sent via email. Memos are internal documents, generally sent from department to department or from a department to a group of people. They are often purpose-driven documents—for example, when a company needs to update its human resources policies. Sometimes memos will be printed and posted on company bulletin boards; other times, memos will be emailed to employees. Memos are written in a particular format, which is shown below.

Assess Your Document Here   **Memo Format & Checklist**

☐⟶ To:
From:
Date:
Re (subject line here, 3-5 words)

☐⟶ Opening Paragraph: State main purpose for writing/reason for writing.
Outline topics and organization of body paragraphs.

☐⟶ **Short, descriptive subhead (if needed)**
Body paragraph 1: State main topic with supporting ideas and details

☐⟶ Body paragraph 2: State main topic #2 (topic sentence) with supporting ideas
and details. As needed, use sub-headings, bullets, in-text citations.

☐⟶ Body paragraph 1: Start with topic sentence. Include supporting information.
Use specific details and in-text citations when appropriate

☐⟶ **Short, descriptive subhead (if needed)**
Body paragraph (if needed):

☐⟶ Conclusion: Restate main point/reason for writing. Include forward looking
statement, reminder of action steps, who to contact for further information/
action (contact statement).

FIGURE 6.6 Memo layout and checklist

7   Email

Email is the most common form of business communication—so common, in fact, that email overload is a serious problem for most people. Studies show workers may spend an average of 28%—nearly thirteen hours—of their workweek on email. Checking email may reduce worker productivity by up to 40%.

For these reasons, writing effective emails is essential. In the deluge of email, you want to make sure your message is read and your information gets to the receiver. Your email reflects on you, your boss, and your company, so presenting a polished, professional image is essential to career success. The following article highlights some of the pet peeves people have about email, ways to write effective subject lines, and ways to manage your email effectively.

After completing this lesson, you will:

- Know and demonstrate use of business email
- Know how to write effective subject lines
- Understand ways to manage email

Reading 7.1

Control That Email! ☺

By Justin Brusino

Manage Your Email

Nearly every person in the business world uses email on a regular basis. But training courses on how to use email properly are uncommon. Many businesses don't instruct their employees in approved email practices, and businesses that do have a set of email guidelines often don't stress their importance.

Email has become the most popular mode of communication in business, and therefore has become a source of stress for many. What is supposed to be a time- and money-saving tool has become a source of frustration and anxiety. Every day we are bombarded with emails that leave us scratching our heads. Why was I sent this? Do I need to know that? What action am I supposed to take? Now, with the popularity of email-enabled mobile devices the frustrations follow us home.

According to Cohesive Knowledge Solutions, a Connecticut-based company specializing in email management, employees now spend more than 40 percent of their workday on email—and most consider more than a third of that time a waste. Wasted time equals wasted money. If your company has all of its employees spending a third of their time on email, how much is being lost in profits and productivity? Regaining control of email is not an impossible task, but it requires some effort and changes in behavior.

This Infoline will help you manage your email more effectively and efficiently. You will learn how to

- develop email etiquette
- increase your email efficiency
- deal with email interruptions
- avoid legal trouble stemming from email.

Use this information to keep your business communication from becoming a headache.

Develop Email Etiquette

As the speed of business increases, so does the speed with which we communicate. The number of emails an employee sends and receives each day is growing every year.

Email is a form of casual communication. It takes little effort to type up a quick question or response and hit "Send." Because of this, it is easy to get sloppy and forget common courtesies. For example, you wouldn't call a co-worker for a favor and neglect to say "hello," and you shouldn't begin your email without a greeting either. Email communications should remain as professional and courteous as other forms of communication. Use the following list of rules, adapted in part from www.emailreplies.com, to help you compose better emails.

- *Be concise*

Do not make an email longer than it needs to be. Reading an email on a computer screen is harder than reading a printed communication, and a long email can be discouraging. Use line breaks to increase white space and to separate information; break important information into chunks, or use bulleted lists. Your email will be easier to read, and your main points will come across more clearly.

- *Answer all questions*

An email reply must answer all questions, and anticipate further questions. If you do not answer all the questions in the original email, you will only receive more emails asking for answers. This will lead to frustration for both you and the sender. When possible, preempt any other questions the sender might have. Doing this will cut down on the amount of email you receive, and will likely impress the sender with your foresight.

- *Use the "Out of Office Assistant"*

It's always a good idea to turn on your "Out of Office Assistant" when you are out of the office training, at a conference, or on vacation. Inform the senders what days you will be gone, whether or not you will have email access, and who else can be contacted for needed information. Assure the senders that you will respond to their email as soon as you can.

- *Use proper spelling, grammar, and punctuation*

When you receive an email with typos, how does that make you view the sender? Sloppy? Lazy? Ignorant? Your emails are being viewed with the same scrutiny. Nothing will make you and your company look more unprofessional than email littered with misspelled words and bad grammar. Not only will you look bad, your message may be unclear and cause a miscommunication.

- *Answer swiftly*

Customers send an email because they wish to receive a quick response. Therefore, each email should be replied to within 24 hours, and preferably within the same working day. You should treat your co-workers' emails with the same consideration as those of your customers. If the message involves a complicated response, answer promptly saying that you received their email and will get back to them. This way, senders won't think that you are ignoring them.

- *Get to the point*

Although it is important to be courteous and include a greeting at the beginning of your email, don't overdo it. Your recipient will be more pleased with a clear, concise message than a list of pleasantries. Keep the small talk to a minimum or include it at the end of the message.

- *Do not attach unnecessary files*

Sending large attachments can annoy your recipients or cause problems to their email system. Try to compress attachments and send only necessary files. Moreover, you need to have a good virus scanner in place so that you do not send viruses to your customers or co-workers.

- *Use proper structure and layout*

Because reading from the screen is more difficult than reading from paper, structure and layout are very important for emails. When making points, number them or use bullets to mark each point as a separate entity.

- *Create a signature*

Your company may or may not require its employees to create a signature that will appear at the bottom of their emails. If it's not required, you should still create one. Include your name, title, and contact information. You might also want to include the company logo, company slogan, and a link to the company website.

- *Use cc: sparingly*

Use the cc: (courtesy-copy or carbon-copy) field only if the recipients know why they are receiving a copy of the message. The cc: field can be confusing because the recipient might not know what action to take regarding the message. In general, do not include the person in the cc: field unless you have a specific reason for wanting this person to see your response. Also, including people in the cc: field too often can clog up their inbox and irritate them.

- *Be careful with bcc:*

Many companies view using the bcc: (blind carbon-copy) field as inappropriate because it hides the recipients' identities. If it is necessary for someone to be included in the message, use the cc: line. Another option is to forward the message to the person separately.

- *Do not overuse the "high priority" option*

If you overuse the "high priority" option, it will lose its function when you really need it. Even if an email is highly important, your message will come across as slightly aggressive if you flag it as such.

- *Do not write in CAPITALS*

WRITING IN CAPITALS MAKES IT SEEM LIKE YOU ARE SHOUTING. This can be annoying and can even cause a misunderstanding and lead to an unfavorable response. The same rule applies to **bolding** or underlining text, which can also be seen as aggressive.

- *Read email before you send it*

A lot of people don't bother to read an email before they send it out, as can be seen from the abundance of spelling and grammatical mistakes found in emails. Using spell check is a good option, but spell check won't find the correctly spelled word in the wrong place. Also, reading your emails through the eyes of the recipient will help you send a more effective message and avoid misunderstandings.

- *Do not overuse "Reply to All"*

More people are guilty of this than they would like to admit. Using "Reply to All" often sends messages to people who do not need to be included. This results in unneeded messages for the recipient. Use "Reply to All" only if you really need your message to be seen by each person who received the original.

- *Do not send emails when angry*

If you are having problems with another co-worker, email can be a tempting way to express your displeasure. Resist this urge. You don't want a record of a personal feud with a co-worker. Take a moment to cool off, then, if you still feel the need to express yourself, talk to the person face-to-face or over the telephone.

- *Take care with email formats*

Be aware that when you send an email in Rich Text or HTML format, the sender might be able to receive only Plain Text emails. If this is the case, the recipient will receive your message as a .TXT attachment.

- *Do not forward chain letters*

Chain letters are hoaxes. Bill Gates will not send you five dollars for each person you forward a chain letter to. Delete these letters as soon as you receive them.

- *Do not request delivery and read receipts*

These will typically annoy your recipients before they even read the message. It also makes it seem like you are checking up on them. If you want to know if an email was received, it is better to ask recipients to reply that they received your message.

- *Do not ask to recall a message*

Most times the message has already been received and read. Instead, it is better to send another email admitting that you made a mistake. You will look more honest and professional than you would if you attempted to recall a message.

- *Use active instead of passive voice*

Use the active voice of a verb whenever possible. For instance, "We will process your order today" sounds better than "Your order will be processed today." The first sounds more personal, whereas the latter sounds unnecessarily formal.

- *Avoid long sentences*

Keep your sentences to a maximum of 15–20 words. Email is meant to be a quick medium and requires a different kind of writing than actual letters. Also, take care not to send emails that are too long. If a person receives an email that looks like a dissertation, chances are that he or she will not even attempt to read it. A good rule of thumb is to keep your email within the length of a computer screen.

- *Do not send offensive messages*

Don't send any emails with any joke or remark that could be taken as sexist, racist, libelous, or offensive. Even if you intend to send the email to one person, it could end up in the hands of dozens and will most likely offend someone. A single remark could mean a lot of trouble for you and your company.

- *Curb the "thank-yous"*

This may sound rude, but more often than not "thank-you" emails do nothing but waste the recipient's time.

These emails are appropriate only when someone really goes out the way to help you. If you are requesting information from someone or asking for something minor, thank the person in advance.

ePolicy Do's and Don'ts

An email policy is a list of guidelines that designates appropriate and inappropriate use of company email, the Internet, and software. Use this list of do's and don'ts, courtesy of Nancy Flynn, executive director of The ePolicy Institute, as a guide when creating or revising your company's email policy.

DO's

- Establish comprehensive, written ePolicies that address employee use of email, the Internet, and software.
- Educate employees about software piracy. Ensure compliance with all software licenses.
- Communicate the fact that the organization's email and Internet systems are to be used strictly as business communication tools. But don't stop there. Provide clear guidance on what is, and is not, considered appropriate electronic business communication.
- Bear in mind that some personal use of your organization's email system may be warranted. For employees who leave the house before dawn and don't return until well past dark, email may be the most efficient and effective way to stay in touch with family members. For the sake of employee morale and retention, savvy employers generally are willing to accommodate their employees' need to check in electronically with children and spouses. Let your employees know where you stand on this issue, and how much personal use (if any) is acceptable.
- Incorporate an overview of your organization's discrimination and sexual harassment policies in your email policy. Because of the relaxed, informal nature of email, some employees will put in writing comments they never would say aloud. Make sure employees understand that regardless of how it is transmitted, an inappropriate comment is an inappropriate comment. And all it takes is one inappropriate comment to land you on the wrong side of an expensive, protracted lawsuit.

- Review your written ePolicies with every employee. New hires and long-time employees, managers and supervisors, full-time professionals and part-time staff, telecommuters and temporary employees, independent contractors and freelancers—everyone should be informed of your email, Internet, and software usage policies. Have all employees sign and date copies of each policy to confirm they have read and understood each document.
- Incorporate your written ePolicies into your organization's employee handbook and new-hire orientation materials. Have the organization's human resources (HR) director review ePolicies with every new employee.
- Address ownership issues and privacy expectations. Let employees know that the contents of the email system belong to the organization, not the individual user. If management monitors and reads employee email, say so. Make sure employees understand that their email can, and will, be read at any time without notice to or permission of the employee. If there is any chance you may want to monitor employees' home computers, make that clear as well.
- Support your email and Internet policies with eWriting and cyberlanguage policies designed to reduce risks by controlling content.
- Establish netiquette policies for email senders and receivers, managers, and staff.
- Implement a risk management policy that incorporates retention and deletion policies, password policies, and monitoring and filtering software.

- Establish a computer security policy. Put into place procedures and tools designed to keep unscrupulous hackers and internal saboteurs out of your system.
- Install software to monitor and filter email and Internet use.

- Purchase cyberinsurance policies to help mitigate electronic risk.
- Develop an eCrisis communication policy for dealing with the media and public should an eDisaster occur.

DON'Ts

- Rely solely on email to communicate your ePolicies. Require each employee to read, sign, and date a hard copy of each policy. Do use email messages, along with the company's intranet system, to remind employees of your policies and management's commitment to enforcing them.
- Expect employees to train themselves. Educate employees about the what's, why's, and how's of your ePolicies. Make employees aware of their eRisks, eRights, eResponsibilities, and the repercussions they will face for violating email, Internet, and software usage policies.
- Create separate policies for management. Establish corporate email, Internet, and software policies, and insist that officers, managers, supervisors, and staff all adhere to them. A supervisor who turns a blind eye to an employee's online gambling addiction, a manager who winks at software piracy, a board member who sends risqué jokes to senior executives—all are putting the organization at risk.

- Forget your international associates. If you do business or operate facilities abroad, incorporate a discussion about effective international eCommunication in your email policy.
- Assign one individual the responsibility of single-handedly enforcing your organization's ePolicies. Make all managers and supervisors aware of the important role they play when it comes to monitoring employee behavior. Assign specific monitoring and enforcement roles to HR and information management professionals.
- Allow employees to dismiss the organization's ePolicies as insignificant or unenforceable. Make sure employees understand that their computer activity will be monitored. Stress the fact that ePolicy violators will face disciplinary action that may include termination. Let employees know you mean business by enforcing your ePolicies consistently.

Effective Subject Lines

Many people make the mistake of ignoring the subject line or using a generic subject. These people fail to realize that the subject line is often the most important part of an email. A successful subject line will ensure your message is read and gets the attention it needs. Remember that the subject line is for the recipient, so it needs to makes sense to the recipient. The subject line should act as a headline and prepare the recipient for your message. Instead of "Requesting Information," try "Requesting Information about Training XYZ." The more specific, the better.

Avoid these vague subject lines:

- Need Help!
- FYI

- Urgent!
- Requesting Assistance
- Thank You.

This guidance becomes even more important regarding co-workers to whom you send messages on a regular basis. A specific subject line will allow the recipient to find your particular message more easily if it needs to be recalled.

If you find yourself replying back and forth with another person on the same message, often the subject of your message will change. Take the time to change your subject line. This way if you need to find the information later, you won't have to search through 20 messages with the same subject.

Email Body Language

Email is a frictionless form of communication. It doesn't allow for the lively back-and-forth communication that a face-to-face or even telephone conversation does. Since email doesn't permit body language or voice inflection, you must choose your words carefully. A harmless, sarcastic comment might end up sounding arrogant or pushy. Read your email carefully, and if a comment has even a slight chance of being misinterpreted, take it out or find another way to say it.

When writing an email, use words that are

- friendly
- courteous
- respectful.

Avoid words that could be construed as

- curt
- demanding
- rude.

It's also important to personalize your emails. This becomes a problem when sending a quick reply, but in general you should always include a greeting and a salutation. If you don't, your message might be seen as selfish and demanding.

References & Resources

External Consultant

Mike Song
CEO and Author
Cohesive Knowledge Solutions
Articles

Gupta, Ashish, et al. "E-Mail Management: A Techno-Managerial Research Perspective." *Communications of the Association for Information Systems,* vol. 17, 2006, pp. 941–961.

Jackson, Thomas, Ray Dawson, and Darren Wilson. "The Cost of Email Interruption." *The Journal of Systems & Information Technology,* vol. 5, no. 1, 2001, pp. 81–92.

Laff, Michael. "The Myth of Multitasking." *T+D,* March 2007, p. 20.

Powell, William. "Email Overload." *T+D,* December 2002, pp. 22–25.

Rudick, Marilynne, and Leslie O'Flahavan. "Email for Good, Not Evil." *T+D,* May 2001, pp. 113–115.

Spira, Jonathan B., and David M. Goldes. "Information Overload: We have Met the Enemy and He Is Us." *Basex,* March 2007.

Weber, Ron. "The Grim Reaper: The Curse of E-Mail." *MIS Quarterly,* vol. 28, no. 3, September 2004, pp. iii-xiii.

Books

Cavanagh, Christina. *Managing Your E-mail: Thinking Outside the Box.* Hoboken, NJ: John Wiley & Sons, 2003.

Chan, Janis Fisher. *E-Mail: A Write it Well Guide.* Oakland, CA: Write It Well, 2005.

Duncan, Peggy. *Conquer Email Overload with Better Habits, Etiquette, and Outlook Tips and Tricks.* Atlanta: PSC Press, 2004.

Flynn, Nancy. *Blog Rules: A Business Guide to Managing Policy, Public Relations, and Legal Issues.* New York: AMACOM, 2006.

———. *The E-Policy Handbook: Designing and Implementing Effective E-Mail, Internet, and Software Policies.* New York: AMACOM, 2000.

Flynn, Nancy, and Randolph Kahn. *E-Mail Rules: A Business Guide to Managing Policies, Security, and Legal Issues for E-Mail and Digital Communication.* New York: AMACOM, 2003.

Overly, Michael R. *E-Policy: How to Develop Computer, E-Policy, and Internet Guidelines to Protect Your Company and Its Assets.* Raleigh, NC: SciTech Publishing, 1999.

Seeley, Monica E., and Gerard Hargreaves. *Managing in the Email Office.* Burlington, MA: Butterworth-Heinemann, 2003.

Shipley, David, and Will Schwalbe. *Send: The Essential Guide to Email for Office and Home*. New York: Knopf, 2007.

Smith, Lisa A. *Business E-Mail: How to Make It Professional and Effective*. San Anselmo, CA: Writing & Editing at Work, 2002.

Song, Mike, Vicki Halsey, and Tim Burress. *The Hamster Revolution*. San Francisco: Berrett-Koehler, 2007.

Steele, Jeffery. *Email: The Manual: Everything You Should Know About Email Etiquette, Policies and Legal Liability Before You Hit Send*. Oak Park, IL: Marion Street Press, Inc., 2006.

Websites

www.emailreplies.com
www.epolicyinstitute.com
www.ewriteonline.com/tools
www.ftc.gov/spam

Assess Your Document Here

Email Format & Checklist

☐ ⟶ Sender's email address
Receiver's email address
Date
    Autogenerated by email program

☐ ⟶ Subject line: 3-5 words

☐ ⟶ Salutation Here:

☐ ⟶ Opening Paragraph: State main purpose for writing/reason for writing. Outline topics and organization of body paragraphs.

☐ ⟶ **Short, descriptive subhead (if needed)**
Body paragraph 1: State main topic with supporting ideas and details.

☐ ⟶ **Short, descriptive subhead (if needed)**
Body paragraph 2: State main topic #2 (topic sentence) with supporting ideas and details. As needed, use sub-headings, bullets, in-text citations.

☐ ⟶ Body paragraph (if needed):

☐ ⟶ Conclusion: Restate main point/reason for writing. Include forward looking statement, reminder of action steps, who to contact for further information/action.

☐ ⟶ Complementary Close,

☐ ⟶ Sender's Name
Email signature block
Position/title
Contact information

FIGURE 7.1 Sample email and checklist

Applying This Skill: Write Email Subject Lines

Write email subject lines for the following emails. There are many possible solutions.

1. A question about what time the test is on Friday, explaining that you lost your printed schedule.

   _____

   _____

   _____

   _____

2. A question about whether or not children are allowed to play ball games in the communal play area. You have seen children playing near the building and fear that they might break the windows.

   _____

   _____

   _____

   _____

3. An email to a book supplier. Your company has run out of stock of a popular book, *Fun Language Exercises*, and you need to order more copies urgently to fulfill increasing orders from customers.

   _____

   _____

   _____

   _____

4. An email delivering a final report that you have completed, requested by the chief of operations two days ago. You have studied the results of a recent product trial and have presented your findings with tables, graphs, and detailed conclusions.

   _____

   _____

   _____

   _____

5. An email answering a colleague's request that you swap shifts next Tuesday. You wish to suggest switching for your Wednesday shift so that you can visit your parents, who live on a boat that is in town from Wednesday to Friday.

   _____

   _____

   _____

   _____

6. An old friend from university is in town and you want to arrange a meeting in the coming week. You are free on Thursday and Friday, and if possible would like to meet near where you work. There is a good cafe nearby called Lou's Diner, where you think it would be best to meet.

   _____

   _____

   _____

   _____

7. A letter of complaint to the manager of a shop where you tried to return some trousers that were too small for you. The staff were rude and did not allow you to return the trousers, blaming you for picking the wrong size. You know the store has a policy that allows you to return any item within twenty-four days, so you wish to both arrange a refund and address the staff's impoliteness.

_____
_____
_____
_____

8. Someone has written to complain to you about a communal drinking area in the office. It has been left in a mess, and the water jug is not being regularly replaced. You have contacted the office manager and decided to put up a sign instructing office members on good drinking-area conduct. Your sign is ready to be put up, and you are writing to both announce these new rules and explain why they are necessary.

_____
_____
_____
_____

9. The mayor is visiting your office, and you are responsible for arranging his transport. There have been complications with the car hire company, however, and you need to suggest to your boss that he use alternative transport options instead. You have compiled a list of chauffeur services, taxis, and public transport choices and are prepared to discuss different options.

_____
_____
_____
_____

*Exercise adapted from Phil Williams via English Lessons Brighton at:
http://www.englishlessonsbrighton.co.uk/*

Assignment: Write a Personnel Report Email

After you complete your team projects, you will submit a personnel report email to your professor. In this case, the personnel report is a reporting and evaluation of each team member's work and participation in the team projects over the course of the semester.

At various times in your career, you will have to provide feedback to peers or subordinates, such as in an annual performance review. Writing honestly, tactfully, and positively is essential to preparing personnel reviews and reports. In this case, the personnel report is a private document between you and your professor (your team members will not read it), but at other times, reports may be shared with other people, and tact is essential.

In this report, you will include the information detailed below. Use standard business email format, including a brief, detailed subject line. Do *not* include the information as an attachment; the email text will be the information.

Send Email

To:
_____

Subject:
_____

Message:

Greeting,

The introduction paragraph will state the purpose of your email. You will mention the assignment you completed, your leadership role, and provide an outline of information to follow in the body of the email.

The body paragraphs will include details about the following:

- Communication: how does your team communicate (group text, in class, email etc.)? How is the group communicating? Are there any issues? If so, explain.
- Working in the team: how is the process so far? Is everyone participating as expected? Are deadlines being met? Explain.
- Meetings: list the date, time, place, duration of, and members present at meetings. Discuss the meeting process; has it been effective?
- Evaluate each team member: provide a percentage score for each team member's contribution to the project.
    - Contribution must be indicated by a percentage and must average out to 100% for the team.
    - Contributions must be in 5% or 10% increments (85% or 90%, not 92.5%)
    - A percentage of 0 must be given to a team member who did not participate
    - See the examples below:

Example 1:

Team Member	Contribution
John	90%
Ali	110%
Shun	100%
Emmy	100%
	400/4

Example 2:

Individual	Contribution
Nischal	110%
Colin	90%
Karlee	110%
Yanran	90%
Chris	100%
	500/5

Write at least 2–3 sentences about each person (including yourself) explaining the rating you assigned each team member. Provide specific, verifiable evidence for each person. For example:

- Ally was present for all of our team meetings and participated actively in our group text. She asked questions when she had them and responded to other team members' questions as well. Ally sent me the required information before the due date and made changes when I asked her to. For these reasons, I assigned Ally a 100% score.
- Sven attended two of our four team meetings; she texted us once to say he wouldn't be there, but the other time, she just didn't show up. Sometimes Sven responded to group texts. She sent me the required information a day after the due date, so I had to spend extra time incorporating her piece into the group project. Overall, I thought Sven could have been more involved, so I gave her an 80% score.

Provide a sense of closure; comment on your team overall and your feelings about working with this team so far, for example. Include a contact statement (whom to contact if the reader has any questions) and close with any goodwill statements as appropriate.

Type your name at the end

Include an email signature block

8   Bad-News Messages

Delivering or receiving negative news is never pleasant, but it's unavoidable. Negative news may be as simple as the inability to attend a meeting or as complex as laying off employees. In most business communications, you put the main point first to save your receiver time and money. But when delivering bad news, you will follow a different organizational format, which is explained below. After completing this lesson, you will:

- Learn and demonstrate the ability to write a bad-news message
- Demonstrate your ability to follow proper message format

Reading 8.1

Persuasive and Bad News Messages

By Janet Mizrahi

Writing Negative or Bad News

Delivering unwanted news is a fact of life in the world of work, and when an organization must inform its stakeholders of negative news, there are basic goals that a message must attain:

- Confirm that the bad news will be understood and accepted
- Deliver the message in a way that the reader will continue to look at the writer or organization in a positive light
- Minimize future contact with the writer or organization about the negative situation

In some cases, delivering bad news uses the direct strategy. For example, anyone who has ever received a rejection letter from a college (certainly bad news!) knows that the bad news comes in the first line. This is done so that the anxious student does not overlook the information. If you think your reader would prefer to read the bad news first or if the situation demands firmness, use the direct approach for bad news. Begin with the bad news itself, explain the reasons for the bad news in the body, and close politely but firmly.

However, bad news is frequently delivered using the indirect strategy. This structure has four main elements, as Table 8.1 illustrates.

TABLE 8.1 Bad news message: indirect strategy elements

Indirect strategy elements	Writing strategy
Neutral or buffer statement	Describe a point on which both parties can agree Express appreciation Begin with good news Offer praise
Reasons leading to message	Include details supporting the denial Omit apologizing Use positive language wherever possible
The negative or undesired news	Clearly state the bad news to eliminate any misunderstanding Deemphasize the bad news by placing it in a subordinate clause
Polite close	Aim to build goodwill by offering an alternative, if possible, or a simple forward-looking statement

Begin your negative news correspondence with a **buffer or neutral statement** about which both the writer and reader can agree: *The recent renovation of the University Club has made it a much sought-after venue.*

Alternately, you may wish to start with a statement of **appreciation**: *Thank you for your well researched proposal to include Mayweather House in this year's Giving Back® volunteer day.*

You can offer any **good news** that is part of the message (as long as it doesn't mislead the reader into thinking the message contains all good news) or offer praise to open your bad news message: *All departments have done a great job decreasing their operating budgets.*

Start the second paragraph of the bad news message by providing logical **reasons** leading to the bad news itself. Slip in the **bad news** in a subordinate clause, and never repeat it. Make sure the negative message is clearly stated so you don't create misunderstanding or encourage further communication. For example, following the previous buffer statement, our next sentence might read:

Since we have expanded our facility to accommodate parties of over 100 and added a gourmet chef, the number of organizations and individuals requesting to use the University Club for events has tripled. Our bylaws require that we give priority to members of the club before opening up our schedule to non-members, so we are unable to accommodate your request to use the Dean's Room on the date you have requested.

The **closing** of the bad news message must be polite and promote goodwill to the reader, who has just heard unwelcome news. Avoid being too conciliatory by offering to provide "additional assistance" or to "call us if you have further questions." If you are able to offer an alternative, do so. For example, if you know that another facility is available to accommodate the faculty retreat mentioned earlier or you can hold it on a different day, say so. If not, simply end on a positive note: *Thank you for considering the University Club for your event, and we look forward to helping you in the future.*

Notes

1 Guffey and Loewy (2015), p. 158.
2 Marsh, Guth, and Short (2012), p. 32.

References

Guffey, M., and D. Loewy. 2015. *Business Communication: Process and Product.* 8th ed. Stamford, CT: Cengage Learning.

Marsh, C., D. Guth, and B. Short. 2012. *Strategic Writing: Multimedia Writing for Public Relations, Advertising and More.* 3rd ed. Upper Saddle River, NJ: Pearson Education.

Applying This Skill: Write a Bad-News Message

As a group, consider the scenario below and the indirect strategy elements discussed in the article above. Plan and draft your message below.

Scenario: At Walding company, a financial services group, you've been helping consumers save for retirement for over twenty-five years. Recently, however, you learned your company computer system had been hacked, and the personal records of nearly all of your customers have been compromised. Write an email telling your customers about the breach and that they may be affected. Develop your message by answering the questions below. Be prepared to share your message with another group.

- How will your audience react to this news?

_____

_____

_____

_____

- What is your neutral opening statement? How can you open with a statement that identifies the topic without sounding negative or too positive?

_____

_____

_____

_____

- What are the issues that led to the bad news? What facts or reasons are relevant to the bad news? How can you give the facts/reasons without sounding negative or too positive?

_____

_____

_____

_____

- What is your bad-news statement? Can you write about the bad news without explicitly stating it?

_____

_____

_____

_____

- What alternative counterproposal or "silver lining" could you offer your audience? How might you use "you" phrases to soften the bad news?

_____

_____
_____
_____

- What is your forward-looking statement? What might you say to maintain a positive relationship between you and your audience?

_____
_____
_____
_____

Draft your bad-news message here:

_____
_____
_____
_____

Assignment: Write a Bad-News Message

Read the scenario below and write a bad-news message, following the principles learned in this section. You may add details as needed.

Scenario: Assume you are the newest sales representative for Weight Loss Clubs, a gym and weight-management company. While the company is about five years old and growing steadily, the president is eager to increase membership and revenues. Because of high real estate rental prices in your city, your club must raise membership rates effective next month. Clubs in nearby suburbs are not subject to the membership rates, but your facility is the flagship club for the company.

Write an email to club members telling them of the membership price increase. Consider the following:

- You do not want to lose members to other clubs.
- Your job depends on your ability to attract and retain memberships.
- You may be noticed for a promotion if you increase memberships.

9   Business Meetings

Some companies hold many meetings—sometimes up to seventy a week! Other companies are doing away with meetings or implementing alternative meeting formats via electronic means, walking, standing, etc. But statistics show there are about three billion meetings held each year. To prepare you for business meetings, we will conduct several business meetings over the course of the semester.

The articles and information below will help prepare you for the business meetings held in class and business meetings you'll attend in the workplace. After completing this lesson, you will be able to:

- Demonstrate the ability to present yourself professionally
- Develop the ability to adapt to changing directions/assignments
- Demonstrate the ability to conduct an interview
- Demonstrate the ability to effectively present information in a group setting

Reading 9.1

Meetings in Academe: It's Time for an "EXTREME MEETING MAKEOVER!"

By Ronald A. Berk

Meeting Diagnostic

Before we blast off, it's probably best to do a quick diagnostic so you don't waste your time reading this article or prematurely skip over it. No skipping yet. You all have different experiences chairing and attending meetings of every size, shape, texture, density, girth, and hue.

Please answer the following five questions about MOST of the meetings you have attended:

1. Do they begin and end on time?
   YES   NO
2. Are they very to extremely productive?
   YES   NO
3. Do they engage most of the persons present?
   YES   NO
4. Do they complete all agenda items?
   YES   NO
5. Are they efficiently run by the chair?
   YES   NO

If you answered "NO" to two or more of those questions, you might want to stay on board and consider the ingredients in a *MAKEOVER*." If you answered "YES" to all of them, it's safe to bail, pass Go, and checkout the other articles in this issue.

What's the Problem with Meetings?

Meetings have a bad reputation with faculty. Rarely do you hear a positive word uttered about an upcoming or past meeting. That reputation has metastasized throughout higher education. The primary reason is because meetings can be major time wasters, accomplishing very little, often deteriorating into just another social event, or they may be the omen for bad news announcements, such as more budget cuts, lay-offs, and furloughs. If you're a social butterfly or other insect, you may look forward to meetings; otherwise, you might endure them as one of the vast numbers of clock-watchers, tweeters, texters, day-dreamers, movie-watchers on your iPhone or iPad, chart-completers, grocery-listers, grant-writers, article-writers or readers, or paper-graders. On more than one occasion, I've contemplated that I would prefer to drink paint (semi-gloss) than sit through another meeting. This reputation and the negative images associated with meetings are well-earned. (*SIDEBAR*: Could this abysmal experience be similar to what students have to endure in some of your colleagues' classes? I hope not.)

Why does this happen everywhere? Several CAT-scan studies of meeting participants typically indicate high levels of brain activity at the start of meetings. After five minutes, brain activity and heart rates decelerate rapidly. What happens? Why are the meetings so boring with frequently so little being accomplished as attendees drift toward ComaLand? It's almost as though there was a DNR sign on the meeting room door.

My preliminary diagnosis is: PUTRID LEADERSHIP!! It's the leader or chair who is totally responsible. Although our colleagues who try to conduct meetings are usually well-meaning professionals from law-abiding families with pit bulls surrounded by barbed wire fences, most of them can't run a meeting properly. This behavior is usually not intentional.

Failure is not premeditated; chairs do not plan to sabotage their own meetings.

The problem is that most administrators, faculty, and clinicians are simply not trained in meeting management. Where do you find "meeting management" taught in any academic curriculum? Meeting management is a business skill, not an academic one. A rather pervasive attitude is: "After all, how difficult could it be to conduct a meeting? Everybody does it." Chairs don't even give it a second thought, much less a first one. You're probably thinking: "It's as easy as nailing a triple axel or quad (if you're a guy) in the Olympic Figure Skating finals." You follow the Nike® slogan: "Just do it!"

(*PERSONAL SIDEBAR*: About a decade ago, I had the privilege of attending a presentation by Stephen Covey [the "*7 Habits*" guy]. He was invited to Johns Hopkins Medical Institutions to address administration issues for the hospital and university staff, including medical faculty, administrators, and staff. One topic covered was how to conduct meetings. As he described the key elements in managing a meeting, there was a lot of rustling in the audience, especially a high incidence of elbow-in-the-ribs jabbing. It was clear that most of us felt we violated and observed our colleagues violating every rule for proper meeting conduct. EVERY RULE!! That was significant. I learned sooo much that afternoon. *End of Lengthy Sidebar*.) We now resume this article already in progress.

Help Is on the Way

Given this ubiquitous problem with meetings, right now I want you to take your previous experiences in conducting meetings or just enduring them and *purge them from your memory*. Lobotomize them completely. Clinically, this is known as a "radical meetingectomy." Let's begin with a clean slate.

According to experts in business and management, there are right and wrong ways to conduct meetings (Harvard Business School, 2006; Henkel & Lujanac, 2007; Hildreth, 1990; Hindle & Heller, 1999; Lencioni, 2004; Smith, 2000; Streibel, 2002; Parker & Hoffman, 2006). In other words, there are "best practices." (*CODE TEAL SECURITY ALERT*: The principles to guide meetings are not hidden in a high-security, top-secret

government installation in Langley, VA. We don't need to hire Jack Bauer of 24 out of retirement to find them, even though he is available since the untimely demise of his counterterrorist program. They have been documented in several books over the past two decades, almost all of which are available as Kindle Editions at Amazon. *End of Teal*.)

If you hop on my rollicking journey through meeting-management world, the time-management benefits will become obvious. Your department doesn't need another putrid leader. There are plenty already hopping around your hallowed hallways. Your institution needs competent leaders who can run meetings effectively and efficiently.

A Baker's Dozen Guidelines: It's *MAKEOVER* Time!

Before you start rollicking or hopping, as a meeting chair, you need to commit to doing your homework. Your preparation for the meeting is the most important

determinant of its success. A baker's dozen, bite-sized guidelines are described next for your "*MAKEOVER*." These bites apply to large faculty or clinical meetings as well as small committee meetings. They are expressly designed to increase your meeting productivity. A few of these were also described by Olson (2010) in the context of collegiality. Here is my 30-year academic spin on the "best meeting practices" from the business experts:

1. Hold the Meeting Only If Necessary

If the information can be disseminated or a decision made without a meeting, cancel the meeting. Meet face-to-face only when the administrators, faculty members, and/or clinicians have to discuss an issue or engage in interaction that could not be effectively achieved online. As you are ready to schedule a meeting, think veeery carefully about whether it is absolutely necessary; then think again. Weigh the alternatives.

Given the increasing multigenerational composition of faculty and staff with GenXers and Net Geners added to the Traditionalists and Boomers, seriously consider "virtual" or Skype meetings. The difficulty of gathering everyone together in one location coupled with the "go-to-meeting" or "mobile" technology for teleseminars and webinars is a viable substitute for in-person, face-to-face meetings and easily accessible to more professionals. It takes traditional conference calls and online chats to another level, plus it can save a lot of in-person meeting time.

2. Invite Only Those Who Need to Attend

Try to restrict your "dream team" total to between five and 10 for most committee meetings involving faculty development planning, curriculum, progressions, promotion and tenure, faculty evaluations, clinical evaluations, research teams, grants, and admissions. This is the optimum range for reaching consensus and making decisions. Faculty senate and other super-sized meetings are a bit more difficult to manage, although these same rules apply. Groups larger than the Mormon Tabernacle Choir can impede the process.

3. Schedule Meetings When Most Participants Are Available

Survey faculty (and students') schedules to determine time blocks during which few have classes or other major commitments, such as watching "American Idol" or "Glee." Try to use those times for most meetings during the semester, if possible. This is an effective "NO EXCUSE FOR NOT ATTENDING" strategy.

4. Prepare a Detailed Agenda with Time Slots for Each Item

Provide specific information on each topic and explain how those at the meeting can be prepared to discuss or vote on an issue. Solicit input on the items and topics or issues that participants want to be addressed. Place the most important items in the middle of the agenda to allow attendees to warm up and arrive. Attach any documents referred to in the agenda so they can be read in advance. Allow a reasonable amount of time for each item to streamline the meeting.

5. Distribute the Agenda at Least a Week in Advance of Meeting Time

Send out the agenda to all participants. Tell them to be thoroughly familiar with all of the items and any support documents. If anyone is presenting an item, he or she should be prepared and cognizant of the assigned time limits. Make it clear that you will hold everyone to their respective time limits to keep the meeting on schedule.

6. Start and Stop on Time

Punctuality is extremely important! DO NOT reward faculty or students for coming in late by recapping what they missed. Instead, they should be horsewhipped in a back room after the meeting. I'm kidding, of course. You can use any room you like. If you do not end on time, attendees may be late for their next meetings, classes, or other commitments. It's a matter of respect for everyone present.

7. Enforce the Assigned Times of Each Agenda Item

Appoint a timekeeper, and make every effort to stick to the schedule. This is the most important time-management technique to get through the agenda on time or earlier. *Think of the agenda as a "to-do" list with all A items.* You must get through every item. Everyone has time limits, even you. Model the use of those limits. Use your discretion to cut off or summarize discussion. Stop filibustering-type wind-bags politely, if necessary. If that doesn't work, gag them with the agenda. They really need to be tasered, but don't do it. Try to keep pace with the original time slots. If you did your homework in preparing this meeting, you should be in control.

8. Don't Permit Agenda-Busting

Don't ask for items to be added to the agenda at the beginning of the meeting. The attendees already had input into developing the agenda. They had their chance. If new, important, and/or urgent items pop up at the beginning or arise during the course of the meeting, they should be (a) dealt with appropriately, (b) tabled until the next meeting, or (c) handled by an ad hoc committee, which can be created to examine the items and report its findings at a future meeting. Use your discretion in handling "emergency" items.

9. Try to Engage Everyone in the Meeting

Each faculty member attending the meeting is there for one of two reasons: Either she volunteered because she's interested and wants to be there and contribute OR he is required to attend. Your responsibility here is meeting management. If there is any shy faculty member or student, draw him or her into the discussion. Ask contentious questions. Play devil's advocate. Find ways to get as many faculty involved and contributing. The meeting should be engaging and interactive for everyone. After all, it's their meeting.

You are there to facilitate the proceedings, but don't let any "trouble-makers" pull the focus of the proceedings. Keep your taser visible. Politely request overzealous, time-eating contributors to meet with you and Guido after the meeting in the back room to discuss their concerns. Quell their zeal by asking them to prepare a written brief or position paper to be attached to the agenda item being discussed. Curb their enthusiasm. Stay in control of the "engagement."

10. Attain Closure on Every Item

Every item should end with a decision based on a vote, referred to a standing or ad hoc committee, or tabled until the next meeting. Nothing should be left hanging.

11. Give a 10-Minute Warning before the Meeting Ends

This is the "bell lap" that every racer hears. Use Pavlov's bell if necessary. It snaps everyone to attention and rivets their eyeballs on the remaining agenda items. Everyone shifts into high gear without meds. The last 10 minutes are turbo-charged. The participants know this meeting must end on the button.

As you wrap up the meeting, right before you end, review the specific tasks the participants are responsible for completing before the next meeting. Make sure everyone is clear on their follow-up job. You might want to send out reminders later after the meeting.

12. Prepare the Minutes and Executive Summary Immediately after Adjournment

Write up the detailed minutes of the meeting and also a one-page executive summary (if appropriate) of the decisions made on every agenda item. The minutes document "what was done" and "who does what next" by a given date; the executive summary simply lists the decisions reached for all items and provides a quick read for those interested who attended the meeting and who did not.

13. Disseminate the Minutes and Executive Summary

Send out both documents as drafts to all participants. While the meeting's actions are fresh in their minds, request their input on additions, omissions, and corrections to the minutes and summary with a clear deadline. After changes are made, send out a final version. Make sure to follow up on the tasks that need to be completed with the faculty and students who were responsible. These tasks should cover all actions taken at the meeting.

Epilogue

If this list raises your consciousness level the next time you plan, conduct, or walk into a meeting, it will be a win-win for you and the participants. If you attend, but do not chair any meetings right now, consider sharing the preceding list with any perpetrator who violates those rules. What do you have to lose?

Further, if you know of students who are having the same problems conducting meetings as your chairs, directors, deans, and faculty, refer them to my student version of meeting hints and protocol (Berk, 2009). Student leaders can benefit from these pointers early in their meeting life and careers to break the meeting mold and help them avert later problems, such as the ones we've encountered. Hopefully, they can contribute to a new and improved generation of meeting chairs.

Finally, meetings should not be perceived as a waste of time, a dreaded appointment in your "to-do" list, or a death walk. They can be opportunities to accomplish meaningful tasks with a positive team-building spirit. If you make the changes recommended in this article, your meetings may even inspire, challenge, and unpack and resolve problems so that everyone grows from the experience of tackling the agenda items together.

"HAPPY MEETINGS, COLLEAGUES!"

References

Berk, R. A. (2009). *The five-minute time manager for college students.* Columbia, MD: Coventry Press.

Harvard Business School. (2006). *Running meetings: Expert solutions to everyday challenges.* Cambridge, MA: Author.

Henkel, S. L., & Lujanac.M. (2007). *Successful meetings: How to plan, prepare, and execute top-notch business meetings.* Ocala, FL: Atlantic.

Hildreth, R. A. (1990). *The essentials of meeting management.* Englewood Cliffs, NJ: Prentice-Hall.

Hindle, T., & Heller, R. (1999). *Managing meetings.* London: Dorling-Kindersley.

Lencioni, P. (2004). *Death by meeting: A leadership fable ... about solving the most painful problem in business.* San Francisco: Jossey-Bass.

Olson, G. A. (2010). How to run a meeting: Conducting committee work as efficiently as possible is a form of collegiality. *The Chronicle of Higher Education*, July 16, A31, A33.

Parker, G. M., & Hoffman, R. (2006). *Meeting excellence: 33 Tools to lead meetings that get results.* San Francisco: Jossey-Bass.

Smith, T. E. (2000). *Meeting management.* Englewood Cliffs, NJ: Prentice-Hall.

Streibel, B. J. (2002). *The manager's guide to effective meetings.* New York: McGraw-Hill.

Ronald A. Berk, Ph.D., is professor emeritus, biostatistics and measurement, and former assistant dean for teaching at The Johns Hopkins University. Now he is a full-time speaker and writer. He can be contacted at rberk1@jhu.edu, www.ronberk.com, and www.pptdoctor.net, and blogs at http://ronberk.blogspot.com.

Assignment: Business Meetings

Over the course of the semester, the class will conduct business meetings. Topics for the business meetings will be distributed during class about a week prior to the scheduled meeting.

For business meetings, you will be evaluated on your content, quality of source (research), and professionalism. Professionalism includes body language (sitting up straight, not fidgeting, etc.), composure, and presentation of information (vocabulary, filler words, etc.).

Each person should be prepared to speak for 2–4 minutes during the meeting. The professor (or TA) will not call on people; it is your responsibility to contribute to the meeting and make your points. You are not required to dress up for the meetings, nor are you required to have visual aids (unless otherwise instructed in class).

An agenda similar to the one below will be distributed about a week before the meeting. It will include details about the topics of the business meetings.

Business Meeting 1 Agenda

Location: Classroom

Date: As assigned

Time: Regular Class Time

Preparation details:

For the business meeting, you will be asked to:

Here is what you need to do:

Presentation details:

Remember, this is a department meeting, not a formal presentation. So, you do not need any visuals, and you do not need to dress up.

We will sit in a circle, as a department would in a conference room. Participants must voluntarily add their information; I will not call on people. In addition to presenting your information, you should ask questions or make comments on other people's topics.

Professionalism is a portion of your score for this assignment. Professionalism includes posture (sit up straight, feet on floor), attention to others (not on phone or computer, paying attention to speaker), tone and clarity of voice (minimal "ums" and "ahs," volume etc.), minimal nervous gestures/repetitive motions (tapping, knee bouncing).

You will be evaluated on the information you present and your professionalism.

Assignment: Interview with a Professional

In this course, we focus on skills you will need when you enter the workforce. We also focus on the job search. The "Interview with a Professional" assignment combines these two objectives by allowing you to network with a professional in your field and make connections between the information you are learning in this course and the way a professional sees communication in the "real world."

For this assignment, you will *identify* a person who is working in the field you want to enter. You will *interview* this industry professional and *report* on the information you learn as assigned by your instructor.

INTERVIEW PROCESS

1. Identify a working professional to interview. If you are an accounting major, try to find someone working in accounting, for example. You may use your current network, LinkedIn, family, or other connections to identify a person to interview, but you may not interview a close family member (parent, sibling, etc.).

2. Set up the interview time/method. Conducting the interview in person is preferred, but you may schedule an interview over the phone, via Skype, or, as a last resort, using email. Give yourself plenty of time to set up the interview time. People are busy, and you need to allow time to schedule the process.

3. Prepare your questions, and bring writing materials to take notes. If you want to record the interview, ask permission prior to beginning. Don't be afraid to ask follow-up questions to clarify points or gather more information that interests you.

4. After the interview, you will present your findings to the class during one of the business meetings.

INTERVIEW QUESTIONS

You will ask the following nine questions. In addition, you may ask two or three additional questions of your choosing. Examples of additional questions appear below, or you may create your own.

1. On average, what percentage of your duties/work is spent on (and how do you use) each of the following:

   - Writing?
   - Reading?
   - Listening?
   - Speaking?

   _____

   _____

   _____

   _____

2. How are communication skills important in your career field?

   _____

   _____

   _____

   _____

3. In the past five years, has the amount/importance of communication increased, decreased, or remained the same for the following audiences:

   - Internal audiences (coworkers, supervisors, board members, etc.)?
   - External audiences (clients, business partners, community members, etc.)?
   - International audiences (clients, partners, politicians, media, etc.)?

   _____
   _____
   _____
   _____

4. How have technological developments in the past 5–7 years revolutionized communication for you, your company, or your industry?

   _____
   _____
   _____
   _____

5. What are the top three technology devices you use? Which of those devices would you be lost without (i.e., cannot go twenty-four hours without)?

   _____
   _____
   _____
   _____

6. Approximately how many email messages do you receive on a daily basis, and what advice do you have for managing the email demands of your job?

   _____
   _____
   _____
   _____

7. What are the top three skills that entry-level employees _need_ in order to succeed?

   _____
   _____
   _____
   _____

8. What are the top three skills that entry-level employees _lack_ or need to improve on?

   _____
   _____
   _____
   _____

9. If you were a student today, what would you do while in college to improve your chances of obtaining a job and succeeding in your first year of employment?

_____

_____

_____

_____

Create two or three additional questions:

10. _____

11. _____

12. _____

IDEAS FOR ADDITIONAL QUESTIONS:

Present Job

- Describe how you occupy your time during a typical workweek.
- What skills or talents are most essential for effectiveness in this job?
- What are the toughest problems you must deal with?
- What do you find most rewarding about the work itself, apart from external motivators, such as salary, fringe benefits, travel, etc.?

Preparation

- What credentials, educational degrees, licenses, etc., are required for entry into this kind of work? Required for advancement into this kind of work?
- What kinds of prior experience(s) are absolutely necessary?
- How did you prepare yourself for this work? What prepared you best for your position?

Lifestyle

- What obligations does your company/work place upon you, outside of the ordinary workweek? Do you enjoy these obligations?
- How much flexibility do you have in terms of dress, hours of work, vacation schedule, workplace flexibility (i.e., telecommuting)?
- Have you changed jobs due to lifestyle choices? Please explain.

Personal Advice

- How well suited is my background for this type of work?
- What do I need to do to become competitive?
- What educational preparation would be best?
- Are there certain majors, minors, or elective classes I can take to improve my chances?
- What kinds of experiences (paid employment or otherwise) would you most strongly recommend?

10   Writing for the Internet and Social Media

With the prevalence of the Internet and the increasing use of social media, writing for those mediums is becoming more and more important. Often, companies will assume new graduates are experienced in writing for the Internet and social media and expect them to have and use those skills. Many of the conventions of business writing that you've learned so far apply to writing for the web and social media. However, these electronic mediums have some particular conventions about which you should be aware. After completing this lesson, you will:

- Understand how social media has changed the communication model
- Understand how people access content on the Internet and via social media
- Know and demonstrate the ability to write for the Internet and social media

Reading & Activity: Jigsaw Activity—Web Writing

This activity combines the "Reading" and "Applying This Skill" activities. Each group will be assigned one piece of the puzzle detailed below. Your group will read the included information, discuss it, and answer the questions assigned. You will be the "experts" for the assigned piece. Groups will then be rearranged so there is one expert on each puzzle piece in each group. In the new groups, each person will "teach" the other group members the information they learned for their puzzle piece. In the end, each student should have a complete picture of the web-writing puzzle.

PIECE #1

1. What is electronic communication? What are its advantages and disadvantages?
2. How has social media changed the communication model?

Electronic communication is anything created and transmitted electronically. It includes documents, texts, files, social media, songs, and videos. While electronic communication is more and more prevalent—93% of documents are created digitally, and only 70% ever migrate to paper—there are still times when you want to use printed documents. You'll use printed messages to:

- Make a formal impression
- Provide legal information like original or notarized signatures
- Protect sensitive information like emailing tax documents or financial information that requires extra levels of security
- Stand out from the flood of electronic messages; it's increasingly difficult to get people to read your messages in a world full of information overload
- Provide a permanent record—it's easier to store electronic documents, but they:
  - need to be updated frequently to maintain accessible file format
  - are sometimes lost due to computer crashes, file corruption, or file deletion
- Read; sometimes it's easier to read complicated documents on paper and share documents with others

Any communication done electronically is electronic communication. This includes:

- Adobe pdf
- Word document
- PowerPoint
- Rss feed

Social media is a form of electronic communication, but not all electronic communication is social media.

Social media has caused a fundamental shift in the way we communicate. It has:

- Transformed passive audiences into active ones
- Caused a shift from old "monologue" model (we talk, you listen) to a "dialogue" model (transparent, authentic, vibrant, consumer driven)
  - Companies are no longer broadcasting a tightly controlled message
- Become about initiating and participating in conversations where people
  - Share content
  - Revise content
  - Respond to content
  - Contribute new content

Users are contributing to conversations and listening to them. This has changed:

- Relationships between companies and stakeholders so they are more dynamic and interactive
- Ways companies are managed, such as marketing strategies
- Behaviors and expectations of consumers and employees

People rely on social media and content sharing to get information that's both personal and professional.

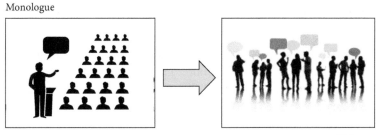

Monologue

Dialogue

FIGURE 10.1

Source: Copyright © 2015 Depositphotos/HonzaHruby; © 2014 Depositphotos/Rawpixel.

PIECE #2

1. How do readers consume content on the web and mobile devices?
2. What is the F pattern, and why is it important?

People read web pages the way they do books in several ways. They read from top to bottom and left to right. Images receive the most attention, and readers use headings to locate information.

But web users don't read large chunks of text. In fact, only 16% of users read online content word by word. They skim and scan. They pick out key words, phrases, and fragments and look for headlines, subheads, and bold text. They pay attention to only some parts of page and are guided by headings, links, and bullet points.

This type of reading is often called "content snacking." This means consumers and readers consume large numbers of small pieces of information. They taste headlines and the first paragraphs of pages.

In one study, researchers tracked the way 232 people looked at thousands of web pages. This study revealed people consistently read web pages in an F pattern.

First, people read horizontally across the upper part of the page. This is typical of the Western style of reading— left to right, top to bottom. This line formed the top part of the F.

FIGURE 10.2   People tend to consume large amounts of small pieces of information from different sources—often social media sites such as Facebook, Twitter, Instagram, LinkedIn, Youtube, and Pinterest.

Next, people tended to move down the page and read in a second horizontal movement. Reading of this second line was typically shorter; this is the second horizontal line in the F.

Third, people vertically scanned the left side of the page. Sometimes this was a slow and systematic movement, which is shown in a solid strip of red on the images. Sometimes, people read faster, which is indicated by the spottier red dots on the vertical axis.

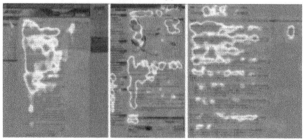

F-shaped reading pattern

(Nielsen, 2006)

FIGURE 10.3

On these images, the red indicates where people's eyes spent the most time. Yellow is second, followed by blue. This tells us people are skimming and looking for information. They are not reading the text thoroughly.

- Fun fact: people read 25% more slowly on screen than on paper.

PIECE #3

Because people read content on the web differently, pages must be written differently.

1. What are some factors to consider when writing for the web?
2. What is the inverted pyramid?

People read 25% more slowly on screens than on paper, and people don't read word for word on screens. They skip around and "snack" on content. Readers approach the web in a nonlinear fashion. It's been described as the difference between a novel and a department store. In a novel, the reader starts on page 1 and reads straight through to the end. The web or mobile readers enter a department store and go directly to the department where they expect to find the content they want.

Because people read differently online, you must write differently for web pages. It means the way you design your page and the way you write has a great effect on whether or not people read and spend time on your page:

- Fun fact: you have about 3–4 seconds to get your readers' attention.

One way to think about delivering content is the inverted pyramid model:

The inverted pyramid is how journalists tend to write; it differs from academic and research writing, which typically has writers lay a foundation with lots of supporting research (base of pyramid) and build to a logical conclusion.

The journalist's inverted pyramid style starts with the conclusion and follows with details. The writer needs to catch readers' attention in the first few words. You start with the conclusion, maybe a summary or 1–2 sentences that give the reader an idea of what the longer piece is about. Then you fill in with supporting information, background, and, finally, details. Basically, your most important information must be first.

You should also limit yourself to one idea per paragraph. You want to use about *half* the word count of traditional writing. A typical Microsoft Word document is about 500 words per page. Google recommends a webpage have between 250-300 words per page. Clearly, conciseness and brevity are even more important than in standard business writing.

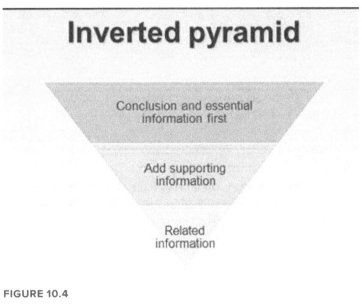

FIGURE 10.4

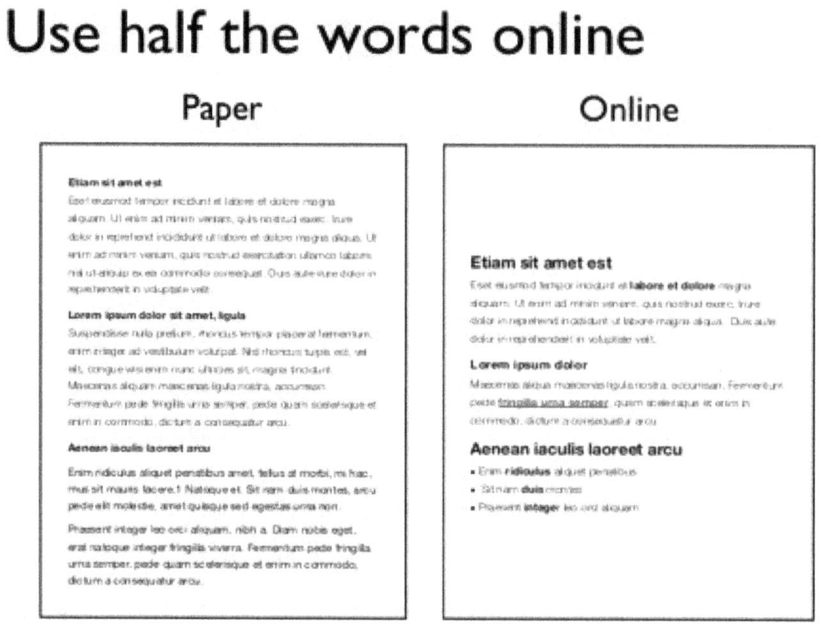

Use half the words online

Paper	Online

FIGURE 10.5 Half words

Finally, in journalism (in newspapers in particular), the old idea was that readers don't look at what's "below the fold," so the most important information was always printed "above the fold." Now, that idea translates to screens. Generally, you can't count on people scrolling beyond the first screen. So, in the first few words and lines, you must focus on key facts and make your main points.

PIECE #4

1. How do you plan to write for the web and social media? (audience)
2. How do you think about content for web pages?

Throughout this class, we've talked about "you attitude" and reader focus. We've talked about being concise and clear. Now, we need to apply these concepts to writing for the web and social media.

Before you write, you have to think about your audience. Who are your visitors? Are they frequent visitors, young or old, casual vs. engaged, technical vs. nontechnical? How would you describe them? Are they busy, curious, and worried? Do they know the subject/company/product? What's their computer/web experience? What's their reading ability?

Knowing your audience will help you tailor your message to different segments. For example, the audience you write for on LinkedIn will likely be different from your Instagram audience, which may be different from your Facebook or blog audience. Consider all of these differences as you are planning what to write.

Next, think about your purpose for writing. Do you want to sell products? Inform people? Tell them how to do something?

Your purpose should align with your business's strategy and goals. The best purposes are specific and measurable. When you write a proposal, what do you want to happen? When you write an email, are you asking for funding or asking people to attend a meeting? If you're writing instructions, what do you want to happen?

After you define your purpose, rethink of it in terms of "you attitude" and your audience. Your purpose should be audience focused and talk directly to reader. You want the audience to:

- Feel involved and identify with your content
- Be part of the conversation

Make sure you're talking to the audience; make them feel engaged, as if they're talking *with* you. This is a conversation or a dialogue, not a monologue.

As with all business documents, readers want to know "What's in it for me?" "Why should I care?" To make sure your pages and content are reader focused, you should use "you" four times more than you use "I" or "we." So, your goal is to:

Not This	This
Sell products	Have people buy products
Inform people	Answer people's questions about ...
Tell customers how to do something	Have people learn to do a task correctly

Lastly, as a web writer, you think about content. Most users get to web pages from search engines, links on other websites, or links within a website. This means pages should be written as if the user hasn't seen the rest of the site. Make sure all relevant information is present (What's relevant? Consider your audience) and make sure your page links easily to other places.

To attract the Internet-savvy audience, your content must be:

- Useful—which means knowing something about your audience. What do they want? What do they know? How can you best give them information?
- Current—Provide the most recent, up-to-date information available, which means constant updating.

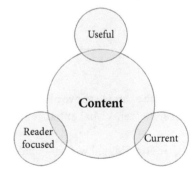

FIGURE 10.6

PIECE #5

1. Explain voice in relation to web writing and social media.
2. How are visual enhancements used in web writing and social media?

When you write, voice describes the personality of writing. Voice is determined by the words you choose, the tone you use, the point of view, and personality. Web and social media are fairly informal types of writing, but informal and casual doesn't mean being sloppy and careless with spelling, grammar, and the like.

In general, you want the voice you use to be personal, friendly, and, ideally, unique. Consider the different voices in the following sentences:

- Web users may subscribe to the free email newsletter below.
- Sign up for your free email newsletter!

Depending on the type of electronic communication, you'll use different voices. If writing for a corporate website, you'll like to use an efficient and informative but approachable voice. An Internet piece would use a less formal voice that is community focused (us, we) and inclusive. Blogs tend to be informal conversations that invite feedback. Before writing or posting, reading previous company posts or competitors' posts will help you identify the appropriate tone to use in each medium.

How would you describe the voices in the examples below?

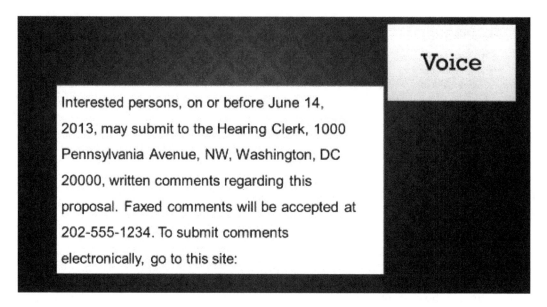

FIGURE 10.7 Voice

The example above also demonstrates the use of visual cues. We've been talking about visual enhancements all semester. Visual enhancements are textual or photo cues to help the reader; they include:

- Highlighted words—bold, italics, etc.
- Bulleted lists
- Headings and subheads to break up text
- Chunking and white space to break up long blocks of text

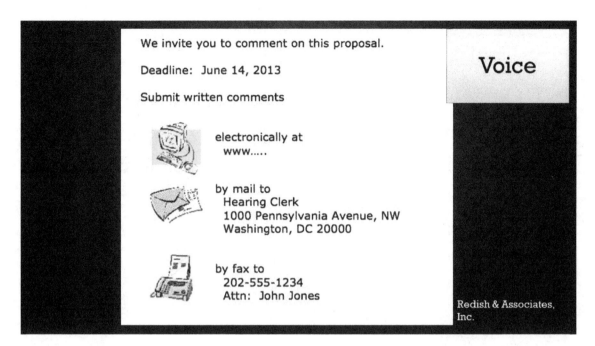

FIGURE 10.8 Voice (2)

These typographical cues help make written text manageable. They create visual separation on the page and draw eyes to specific sections.

Consider the following examples:

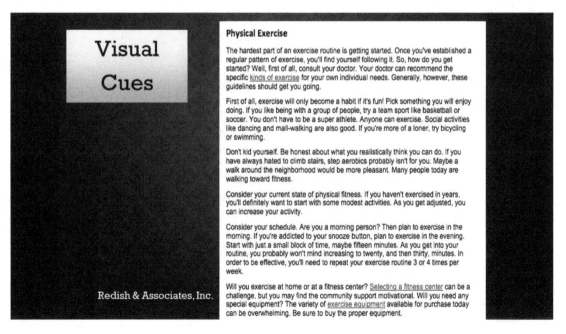

FIGURE 10.9 Visual Cues

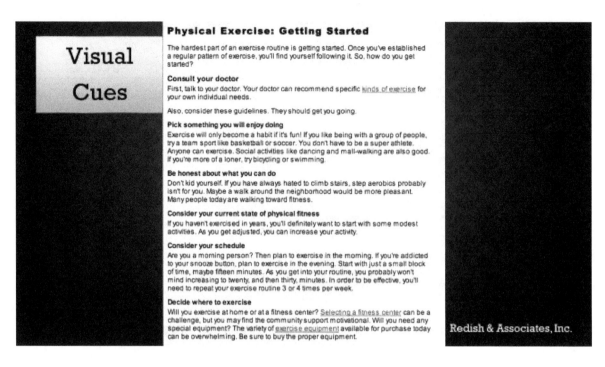

FIGURE 10.10 Visual Cues (2)

PIECE #6

1. Why is writing concisely important in web writing and social media?
2. Why are verbs important in web writing? How are they used?

In all business communications, concision and brevity are important. Web writing should have about half the word count of conventional writing. As a general guideline:

- Headlines—eight words or less
- Sentences—12–20 words
- Paragraphs—40–60 words; 2–3 lines

One way to be concise is by headlining. Headlines are short, specific, concise statements that get the main point across in just a few words. People tend to read the headlines, so this is your chance to capture your readers' attention. As information overload becomes more and more problematic, effective headlines become more essential. Your headlines need to:

- Be short, specific, concise, and informative—people are "snacking" on information
- Include keywords that will be found by search engines—keywords are terms or phrases (usually 2–3 words) your customers would likely use to describe your products or services
- Make sense on their own—they may be all the audience reads, so make them clear and memorable without being too cutesy

Consider the headline examples below:

FIGURE 10.11 Pen

Source: website screenshot: © DBA Products.

FIGURE 10.12 Bird

Source: https://bench.li/images/5845.

Some of the most effective headlines include verbs. In audience-focused content, talking directly to the reader makes them feel involved and part of the conversation. The verbs tell the audience what you want them to do. The web audience often wants direction: What should they do next? Do you want your audience to take a quiz, set up an appointment, or download a free worksheet? Do you want them to take action on the site? After they leave the site?

Consider the two examples above. How do they use verbs and calls to action? How does that work with the headlines?

Applying This Skill: Jigsaw Activity for Writing for the Internet and Social Media

Piece #1

- What is electronic communication? What are its advantages and disadvantages? When should you use paper communications?

  _____
  _____
  _____
  _____

- How has social media changed the communication model? Explain the monologue vs. dialogue models of communication.

  _____
  _____
  _____
  _____

Piece #2

- How do readers consume content on the web and mobile devices?

  _____
  _____
  _____
  _____

- What is the F pattern, and why is it important?

  _____
  _____
  _____
  _____

Piece #3

- *What are some factors to consider when writing for the web?*

  _____
  _____
  _____
  _____

- *What is the inverted pyramid?*

  _____
  _____
  _____
  _____

Piece #4

- How do you plan to write for the web and social media? (audience)

  _____
  _____
  _____
  _____

- How do you think about content for web pages?

  _____
  _____
  _____
  _____

Piece #5

- Explain voice in relation to web writing and social media. Give an example of different voices.

  _____
  _____
  _____
  _____

- How are visual enhancements used in web writing and social media?

  _____
  _____
  _____
  _____

Piece #6

- Why is conciseness important in web writing and social media?

  _____
  _____
  _____
  _____

- Why are verbs important in web writing? How are they used?

  _____
  _____
  _____
  _____

Summing Up Unit II: Formats

After completing Unit II: Formats, you have an understanding of the standard business communication formats. Using these formats appropriately will ensure you present your best self in the workforce. After completing Unit II, you should be able to:

- Format and write effective business letters, memos and emails
- Write bad news messages
- Present yourself and information at a business meeting
- Understand the characteristics of writing for the Internet and Social Media

You may want to review the formats as the course progresses. For example, when completing Team Project 2: Social Media Audit, you may want to review the guidelines and suggestions about writing for the Internet and Social Media. The formats and stylistic elements learned in this unit should be used throughout the course and in the business world.

Preparing to Apply for a Job

- ▶ LinkedIn
- ▶ References and Resumes
- ▶ Cover/Job Application Letters
- ▶ Interviewing

As you near the end of your college career, you will be looking for a job. Finding a job can be a huge undertaking, requiring a lot of time, effort, and attention to detail. In Part Three, we will focus on a variety of skills that will help you stand out when applying for a job. You will learn about LinkedIn, writing a reference page, resume, and cover letter, and interviewing skills. Competition in the job market is fierce, but after completing this section, you will be prepared to find your ideal job.

Reading 11.1

These Are the Skills Bosses Say New College Grads Do Not Have

By Karsten Strauss

As college graduates burst out of the gates of their respective alma maters, polished and confident in their abilities, few are probably thinking ahead to a possible speed bump that sits in their paths. That stubborn obstacle would be the disconnect between the jobs they eventually secure and the skills they've learned thus far.

The gap has always existed. Young people coming out of school cannot all be expected to immediately possess the hard skills organizations require. Some will, of course, but most won't. To get a better grasp on what exactly new entrants to the workforce are missing, online benefits and compensation information company, PayScale, surveyed 63,924 managers and 14,167 recent graduates earlier this year. The results they turned up are pointed.

PayScale's report—taken from data acquired as part of the organization's larger employee compensation survey—shows that certain soft and hard skills tend to be missing from young graduates.

Among 'hard skills'—unambiguous proficiencies useful on the job—managers said new grads were most lacking in writing proficiency. In fact, 44% of managers surveyed said as much. Also, 39% of managers found their recently matriculated hires to be lacking in public speaking skills and 36% claimed they needed to bone up on their data analysis talents—that includes knowledge of programs like Excel, Tableau, Python, R, etc.

Among soft skills, managers were even more united in their opinions of where they see a dearth. According to PayScale's survey, 60% of managers claim the new graduates they see taking jobs within their organizations do not have the critical thinking and problem solving skills they feel are necessary for the job. Additionally, 56% of managers said recent grads do not pay attention to detail and 46% said the young workers would do well to hone their communication skills. Some 44% of managers reported a lack of leadership qualities and 36% reported lower-than-needed interpersonal and teamwork skills.

That managers feel the latest additions to their organizations need to develop some further skills may not be entirely surprising. On the other side of the table, though, recent graduates seem to feel—for the most part—that they are going into their new gigs reasonably prepared.

According to PayScale's survey, 25% of recent grads felt they were "extremely prepared" for their new jobs while only 8% of managers agreed. 62% of recent grads felt they were "mostly prepared," while only 42% of managers concurred. When asked whether they were "well prepared," 87% of recent grads said they were, but only 50% of managers seemed to feel that way.

The gap between the skills college grads have and what they need to succeed at their new careers is very real. Luckily the chasm can be bridged by some added instruction and earned experience.

11   LinkedIn

LinkedIn has become the largest professional networking site, with about 467 million total users and 106 million active users every month communicating in twenty-four different languages. LinkedIn has over three million active job listings, and hiring managers and recruiters are constantly looking for desirable candidates (Chaudhary, 2017).

Creating an effective profile on LinkedIn has been written about extensively and is reviewed in the article below. Here, the goal is to encourage you to use LinkedIn. Recruiters and hiring managers are more likely to see your profile and be interested in the skills and talents you have to offer if you are actively using LinkedIn.

Once you have an excellent profile, you need to actively use LinkedIn. Recruiters are most likely to spot people who are engaged and active on LinkedIn. The following activities will help you become active on LinkedIn. After completing this lesson, you will:

- Know how to share articles, photos, or videos on LinkedIn
- Connect with an alumnus to increase your network
- Understand how to request a recommendation
- Demonstrate your ability to recommend someone
- Network with other professionals

Reading 11.2

Using LinkedIn to Connect

By Kimberly Schneiderman

LinkedIn is a powerful professional networking tool. It is designed to bring people together, expand networking circles, and empower users to exchange information.

However, this powerful tool can be a mystery for some people. They don't have a full understanding of its use and how it can be leveraged effectively in a job search for research, networking and outreach, and self-marketing.

In addition, people often think of LinkedIn as only a place job seekers go when they are looking for a job. While it is true that LinkedIn does have a strong pull for job seekers, it is smart for anyone that is seeking to advance their career in the long-run, trying to sell a product or idea, or seeking to connect with fellow experts to stay active on LinkedIn. LinkedIn is a networking site that opens a world of opportunity for anyone with both short- and long-term career goals.

Basics on LinkedIn

A user can leverage LinkedIn to connect with people they know to ask advice, ask for information, inquire about an open position they saw advertised, or conduct research on a company or its employees. Some main ideas to understand about LinkedIn are:

- Picture: Analysis has shown that pictures with an open mouth smile and a slight head-tilt are the best pictures.

- Headlines: By leveraging the headline statement to communicate one's professional expertise, a user shows that they are career-focused, not just an employee of a company.
- Short Paragraphs: By limiting paragraphs to 2–3 sentences, information will stand out better and readability of the profile will be enhanced.

- "I" Language: Because LinkedIn is a networking site, it is meant to be supplemental to a live conversation. All users of LinkedIn should write the profile using "I" language rather than in resume style or third person to come across in a friendly, personable—yet professional—manner.
- Connections: There are no rules about who makes a good connection. A user can connect with professors, colleagues, peers, managers, supervisors, co-workers, clients, vendors, friends, and, as the Sesame Street song goes, "the people that you meet each day."
- Quantity of Connections: The more connections one has, the easier it is for that person to be found by a recruiter or hiring manager that is conducting a search based on key words.

Natural Networking Ideas that Work

Some people are naturally good at networking and treat it as a way of life. They easily start conversations, seem to know someone wherever they go, and often make connections for the benefit of others. All professionals can learn from these people, no matter if the focus is on landing a new job or simply expanding their network. Here are several practices those natural networkers seem to use:

- Invite Conversation: People who "know everyone" seem to invite conversation; they ask about peoples' children and their jobs, and they are interested in talking about topics that most people know something about—top news stories, seasonal events, or kids' activities.
- Remember Details: By remembering details about other people, one can ask others specific questions like, "How is Janie enjoying college life?" or "How is your new job going?" People feel important when others remember things about them.
- Reach Out: Once a person starts taking in more information about other people, they will naturally find more reason to reach out to them via email, LinkedIn messaging, or phone. A person can send an article they think a contact at their target company may interested in reading, they can share an idea for an industry expert that can help their contact with a project, or simply say how great it was to talk with a new contact.
- Share: When one is seeking to expand their professional reach or is in an active job search, it is not the time to be tight-lipped. It is important to share professional goals and talk about aspects of one's life beyond work. By being open about professional goals and focus, it opens opportunity for others to offer help.

These ideas are important for anyone seeking to network with people both on LinkedIn and through external situations, like industry conferences, business meetings, chance encounters, networking meetings, and special events.

LinkedIn's Advanced Search Function

One of the tools LinkedIn has created that is particularly useful to job seekers and for those seeking to network is the Advanced Search function. With this function, a user of LinkedIn will be able to look for a person with a very common name and tie them to a specific company; they may even be able to find a person with a specific position within a company at a specific location. The advanced search function is extremely useful when one is conducting an aggressive job search and may be doing a good deal of outreach.

In the search bar, a user can search on a person's name, job title, or company name. The Advanced Search function (Figure 2) opens the option to search for combinations of information. This type of search is also referred to as a "Boolean search." To use the Advanced Search function, click on the word "Advanced" next to the standard search bar. Once the selection is made, the Advanced People Search window opens.

Now a user can search on a host of keywords, people's names, job titles, company names, and locations. The data can be filtered by degree of relationship and multiple other options that will help target specific results.

Those results can then be used to help a professional or job seeker identify people they wish to contact. In the following sections is information and suggestions on what can be said and what can be asked of those contacts.

Specific Requests and Communications

An area in which people often do not represent themselves well is the request for specific help and communicating specific information. While there is likely a host of psychological reasons people in are shy about this, the bottom line is that the more specific the information offered or request given, the easier it is for others to fulfill that request and understand one's goals.

This is especially true for people in a job search. Job seekers are often in need of information, resources, introductions, or other help, yet do not ask for it directly for fear of coming across too aggressively or closing themselves off to opportunities. The reverse is actually true. By communicating specifically, the job seeker comes across as focused and confident, and it ensures their intentions are understood, and it gives the other person precise and actionable requests they may be able to fulfill quickly.

Specific requests or communication messages may include:

- Information about a company or a person's industry experience in addition to professional and educational background.
- Introductions to a key hiring manager, recruiter, or other influential person.
- Pre-interview research on the history of a company or a position, or data on the company or specific products.
- Advice and insights on job search strategy and goals.
- Resources and recommendations for deeper learning that may include seminars, books, trade journals, and courses.
- Self-marketing and request for consideration in response to an application.

These communications can appear in a variety of ways for a job seeker. Sometimes the messages come easily; other times, a job seeker may find it hard to figure out what to say. Here are examples to help a job seeker formulate what they wish to say:

- Asking for an informational meeting: Hi Jenna, it was great bumping in to you last week. I was hoping I could spend a little more time with you. I'm changing my career path right now and am focused on the [industry or field] and thought you might be able to share your experience working with [name of company or industry]. Could I buy you a cup of coffee next week or could we set up a time to talk via phone?
- Asking for an introduction: Hi Greg, I noticed on LinkedIn that you know [person's name] at [name of company]. Would you be able to introduce me to them? I saw an open position at the company that fits my experience and skill set to a "T," and I would like to make a connection there to learn more.
- Asking for information on a company: Hi John, I was hoping you and I could connect early next week. I have an interview with your firm, XYZ Company, in the research department for a consumer research manager position. I want to be sure I market myself well and was wondering if you would have 20 minutes time to discuss the company's current focus and recruiting processes with me?
- After applying to a job: Hi Jane, I recently applied for the open [Title of Job] position and wanted to reach out to you to introduce myself. Jeff Jones, marketing manager at your company, gave me your contact information; he and I worked closely together from 2010–2015 and he recommended I contact you directly. Three distinct skills I possess that will be an advantage in the position are [Skill 1, Skill 2, and Skill 3]. In past positions, I've been able to leverage these skills to help the company achieve results that include [quantifiable results]. I welcome the opportunity to talk with you about the position and how my experience aligns with your needs. Thank you for your consideration.
- After applying to a job (to a recruiter or hiring manager via LinkedIn): I've just applied for the Operations Mgr spot (Req #12345) that you posted. I invite you to review my profile and welcome the chance to speak with you about the position. *This message is 140 characters—the perfect length for the Personalized Invitation message on LinkedIn.
- LinkedIn connection request to past colleague: Hi Jeff, hope all is well. It has been almost 7 years since we've spoken—it's about time we reconnect! Your career path looks great; can't wait to hear all about it. *This message is 134 characters—giving you 6 more characters to use for the Personalized Invitation message.

- Asking for advice: Hi Helen, great to hear from you! Actually, I'm in transition right now. I'm pursuing a change and am focused on landing a new [Title of Job] position. I'm looking to leverage my 10 years of experience in [description of work] to really create an impact in the area of [corporate goal or objective]. In fact, you may be a good person to connect with. I'm trying to better understand [insert area of advice needed] and would love to get your input on that. Could we set up a coffee date or phone call later this week?

What If's of LinkedIn

What if a person doesn't respond to a connection request or to an email sent on LinkedIn? This happens frequently. There is no way to predict the follow-through habits or level of use of LinkedIn of another person. In this case, the user can resend the email or try to reach out to the person via regular email to launch a conversation.

What if a person cannot be found on LinkedIn?

Some people simply have not joined LinkedIn yet. A job seeker could try using a Google search to locate a person's contact information or seek out their other contacts and colleagues to obtain an email address or phone number of the desired person.

What if someone unknown requests to connect?

There are different schools of thought on this. Some people will decide outright not to connect with anyone they haven't already met; others will simply respond to the request with "Thank you for reaching out. What was your motivation for contacting me? How can I help?" Some LinkedIn users have decided to be open networkers and accept any invitation they receive. No matter what the decision, be sure to have a deeper conversation with anyone requesting a connection. Engage the person in a quick conversation and see if there are shared interests or needs.

What if an endorsement is given for a skill not possessed?

Endorsements are easy to give. All one has to do is a few clicks and they can praise another person for a bevy of skills that they may or may not possess. The jury is out, but leaning toward the negative, on the power of endorsements since they are so easy to obtain. The bottom line is that for most people, the legitimately-held skills will rise to the top of the list and they ultimately communicate what skills one truly does possess. A user has the option of approving the endorsements or deleting endorsements they do not want to appear on the list.

What if a person writes a recommendation; is it more powerful than an endorsement?

They can be more powerful if the recommendation is sincere and specific. The person leaving the recommendation should comment on projects they have worked on with the user or specific management styles and skills the person possesses. Recommendations can be given by former managers or colleagues, peers, vendors, clients, or co-workers, among others. However, recommendations shouldn't be tit-for-tat or part of a self-promoting strategy. It looks suspicious if two people leave similar recommendations for each other.

Remember, It Is Not All About Taking

When people think of networking—either on LinkedIn or in everyday life—they often think of what they can get out of the outreach, as if it is a transaction. Networking shouldn't be a one-way street. In a networking situation—whether it is a conversation with a neighbor or coffee with a colleague—if a person pays attention to opportunities to give in the meeting rather than just focusing on what they can get, they will come across as someone that cares and is intrinsically focused on others' success in addition to their own.

Here are a few ideas for ways to contribute during a networking meeting:

- Make an introduction to a colleague who can help the networking contact. Perhaps one knows a consultant or subject matter expert for a project the contact is launching.
- Refer a candidate for an open position (a job that isn't right for the job seeker, of course) that the contact is seeking to fill.
- Offer information about or a key contact at a company with which the person is seeking to do business.
- Provide a reference for a job candidate; comment on the candidate's skills and experiences as they align with the job requirements.

- Share experiences from the job search with a contact who is also seeking new employment. Include information on what has worked well in networking, interviewing, and outreach.

This approach to networking doesn't mean the exchange will always be one-for-one, but it does show the contacts that the job seeker or networker is willing to contribute as much as they can. In advance of any meeting or outreach, the person can think of a few ways they might be able to give, not just receive.

Wrapping it Up

LinkedIn is designed for business networking. It doesn't require hours of attention and isn't meant to be a social outlet or a site with content that changes from minute to minute. Among its many uses, it is meant to be a place that a user can go to connect with peers and others in the interest of pursuing career aspirations or just maximizing one's professional reach.

No matter what one's level of use is with LinkedIn, it is important to have a presence so that when the time comes for more aggressive networking (i.e. when a person enters a job search or has important connections to make), the person isn't starting from scratch. By using LinkedIn on a regular basis to connect with colleagues, reach out with quick notes to touch base, or to connect with industry experts, a person will be able to count on those relationships in times of need.

Recommended topics to research on LinkedIn include building the profile, networking through groups, leveraging others' connections, posting articles, following companies, communicating through the messaging feature, and using the job board, among other topics.

Enjoy networking!

About the author

Kimberly Schneiderman is currently a Practice Development Manager with the innovative outplacement firm, RiseSmart. In her role, she develops content, programs, and training courses for both job seekers and the company's coaches. She hails from the career services industry. In 2003 she launched her own resume writing and job search coaching business after what can only be called an "Aha! Moment" with a friend seeking a new job. Through the years, she built a specialty practice working with senior level officers from several law enforcement sectors as they sought to transition to the private sector. In addition, she has worked with professionals and executives from fields of fraud prevention and protection, technology, finance, research, law, sales and marketing, and other areas. Throughout her years in the industry she has developed numerous tools including guides for resume and cover letters, LinkedIn, interviewing, networking, skill building, and even entrepreneurial pursuits. She has also presented on those same topics at professional industry conferences, on client-facing webinars, and onsite for corporate customers. She has authored numerous career-related articles and videos, and has appeared on news and radio programs as a subject matter expert. She has held various board positions with the National Resume Writers' Association and is currently the Certification Committee Chair for the organization. She has attained certifications in resume writing, leadership coaching, and interview strategies, and is a member of the National Resume Writers' Association and an associate with Career Thought Leaders. She earned the Bachelor of Science [Business] in 1997 a Saint Cloud State University G.R. Herberger College of Business.

Contact her as follows:
Kimberly Schneiderman
RiseSmart
South Orange, New Jersey USA
917-584-3022
Web site: www.risesmart.com

Assignment 1: Sharing Ideas, Questions, Articles, and Links

For Assignment 1, you will post and comment on an article, link, video or idea. In this assignment, you are not writing an article. You will post content, summarize it, and comment on it.

From your homepage:

1. Sign in to your LinkedIn account.
2. At the top of your homepage, click the "Share an article, photo, video, or idea" field.
3. Type your summary and comment into the text box. Attach the URL link for the article on which you are commenting.
4. Click "Post."

From a partner page:

1. Sign in to your LinkedIn account.
2. On the article page, click the LinkedIn icon and complete the following options.
3. Click share.

Remember to include your own summary and comment.

Assignment 2: Requesting Advice from an Alumnus

For Assignment 2, connect with an alumnus from you school using the LinkedIn search or groups features. Ask that person for some advice about your career search, your field of study or the person's career path. Alumni are usually happy to help students from their alma mater.

1. Sign in to your LinkedIn account.
2. Locate an alumnus working in the field or at a company where you would like to work when you graduate.
3. Send a message to the alum to introduce yourself and ask a question.
4. Make a screen capture of the sent message (and responses, if you receive any before the assignment is due).
5. Submit the screen capture electronically.

Assignment 3: Asking for a Recommendation

For Assignment 3, you will ask someone to recommend you on your LinkedIn page. Recommendations are important to help recruiters see and value your skills.

1. Sign in to your LinkedIn account.
2. Identify a coworker, mentor, friend, etc. who may write a good recommendation for you. On your connection's profile page, click the "More" icon in the top section of the profile.
3. Select "Request a Recommendation."
4. Fill out the "Relationship" and "Position at the time" fields.
5. Add a short comment (2–4 sentences) that personalizes your message. Explain your situation and remind the person of where you worked together. Be gracious, and say thank you.
6. Make a screen capture of the request.
7. Submit the screen capture electronically.

NOTE: This recommendation activity is not the same as endorsing someone's skills on LinkedIn.

Assignment 4: Writing a Recommendation

For Assignment 4, you will write a recommendation for someone you know. Consider recommending a co-worker, classmate, committee or organization member. Write a brief paragraph or two explaining the person's skills and talents.

1. Sign in to your LinkedIn account.
2. Identify a coworker, mentor, friend, etc. who you want to write a recommendation for. On your connection's profile page, click the "More" icon in the top section of the profile.
3. Select "Recommend."
4. Fill out the following prompts.
5. Personalize the message by entering text in the message field.
6. Make a screen capture of the recommendation.
7. Submit the screen capture electronically.

12   Job Application Documents: References and Resumes

When applying for a job, two of the essential documents are a reference sheet and a resume. A reference sheet lists the names of people a company may call to ask about you: your performance, personality, traits, and habits. You will want to carefully select the people you list as references and carefully format your reference sheet. A resume is a brief summary of your educ ation, experience, skills/accomplishments, and activities. A perfect resume is essential to getting an interview with a company. Many recruiters will eliminate your resume based on a single spelling or grammar mistake. It is important that these documents be perfect so you shine as the great candidate you are. After completing this lesson, you will:

- Identify people to act as references
- Have created a professional reference sheet
- Identify elements of a professional resume
- Have created a professional resume

Assignment: Job Application Packet

One goal of this course is to help you have a completed job application packet ready to use for internship or job searches. By the end of the course, you will have a professional:

- Resume
- Reference sheet
- Cover/job application letter

The activities in Chapters 12 and 13 will help you prepare your job application documents. As assigned by your professor, submit the documents listed above and your internship or job posting to complete the Job Application Packet Assignment. (Save the job posting; you will need it several times during the course.)

   The Job Application Packet assignment will collect all of your job application documents into one portfolio. After receiving feedback on your reference sheet, resume, and cover letter, you should make changes and edits before submitting the final documents in the Job Application Packet. The final Job Application Packet will include:

   o   Reference Sheet
   o   Resume
   o   Job Application/Cover letter
   o   Copy of the job advertisement/posting to which all documents are targeted

Reading 12.1

Enhance Your Writing with Graphic Elements

By Paul R. Timm and Sherron Bienvenu

Four Basic Design Principles

As we develop graphic elements in our documents, we need to be aware of four key principles:

- Contrast.
- Repetition.
- Alignment.
- Proximity.

Contrast

Contrast has to do with the variances in such things as typefaces (fonts) and other graphic elements. The simple rule for effective contrast is that it must be significantly distinctive. If, for example, you wear a navy blue blazer with dark grey slacks, you are not showing much contrast. In fact, people may have to look closely to see if they are really different colors. The same navy blazer with khaki slacks exhibits dramatic contrast. In other words, contrast needs to be significant. Little contrast provides no advantages. Look, for example at the two business cards below. Which grabs your attention better?

Contrast needs to be significant, not subtle.

Influential Consulting
Adam W. Young

916 Old River Road
Buffalo, NY 14602
(801) 422-1212

Influential Consulting
Adam W. Young

916 Old River Road
Buffalo, NY 14602
(716) 555-1212

Examples of Contrast in Design.

On a simple list, contrast in fonts can help categorize ideas for better reader comprehension. The list below illustrates this.

List without contrast:

CD ROMs
—Children's CDs
—Educational CDs
—Entertainment CDs
Educational
—Early learning
—Language arts
—Science
—Math
Teacher Tools
—Books
—Teacher guides
—Videos

Same list using simple contrast to categorize:

- **CD ROMs**
  Children's CDs
  Educational CDs
  Entertainment CDs
- **Educational**
  Early learning
  Language arts
  Science
  Math
- **Teacher Tools**
  Books
  Teacher guides
  Videos

Although this principle is simple, it can be a powerful way to enhance reader comprehension. To recap, apply these principles to create graphic contrast:

- Avoid elements on the page that are merely *similar.*
- If the elements (type, color, size, line thickness, shape, space, etc.) are not the *same,* make them *very* different.
- Contrast is often the most important visual attraction on a page.

Repetition

The second basic design principle is repetition. This element involves consistency of design. Check documents to be sure they:

- Repeat the same *visual elements* of the design throughout the piece.
- Repeat color, shape, texture, spatial relationships, line thicknesses, sizes, etc.
- Use repetition to develop the *organization*, strengthen the *unity*, and add *visual interest*.

Inconsistent design and layout distracts readers and damages your professionalism. Always re-check visual elements and ask for feedback from others. Specifically, ask a trusted associate (preferably one with an eye for detail) to review your document checking for consistency.

Alignment

Be conscious of where you place elements on the printed page. Find something to align with. If you have a graphic or illustration, consider how text should be associated with it. You may choose to "wrap" around an illustration or use a standard point of "justification" (the margin line your text follows). Word-processing software provides four choices in justification: left, center, right, or "full" (which aligns both left and right by adding spaces as needed to fill out the line).

Avoid using more than one text alignment on the page (don't center some text and right-align other text). Also, use center justification sparingly. It can be effective but often comes across as unimaginative, harder to read. The ad for construction workers shown below uses center justification (among other design flaws) and appears busy and confusing.

An Example of Bad Alignment.

See how this same ad could be cleaned up using better justification and eliminating unnecessary graphic elements:

An Example of Good Alignment.

The other rules for alignment can be summarized as follows:

- Nothing should be placed on the page arbitrarily. Think about ease of reading, consistency, and appropriate contrast.
- Alignment creates a clean, sophisticated, fresh look.
- Every element should have some visual connection with another element on the page.

This last point leads to the final basic design element, proximity.

Examples of Good (bottom) and Bad (top) Proximity.

Proximity

Readers often need to be shown how points in your document relate to each other. Proximity involves grouping related items close together. These grouped items then become one visual unit rather than several separate units. This helps organize information and reduces clutter.

To illustrate the principle of proximity, look at the two advertisements below. The first does little to group elements, making it difficult for the reader to dig out the meat of the message. The second uses the principle of proximity to associate related information.

The design ideas we have shared in this section are, of course, very basic. If you produce documents requiring more sophisticated design, we encourage you to involve professional artists. That said, these ideas can improve even your routine documents. Keep in mind the four principles of contrast, repetition, alignment, and proximity (you can make that into an acronym if you like!), and you will enhance the impact and professionalism of your written documents.

Reading 12.2

Line Up Your Personal and Professional References

By Diane Huth

Every employer is going to ask for references, so be prepared with a list of both personal and professional references before an employer asks for them. They will include your mentors, plus current and former employers, colleagues, vendors, customers, professors, colleagues from organizations you volunteer with. Select people who will write and say glowing things about you. Before you actively start your job search, call or talk with each of your mentors and ask if they will be willing to serve as a reference for you.

Once your mentors say yes to serving as a reference, make sure you have their contact information, which includes name, title, phone number, email and physical address. Create a nicely-formatted Word document with your contact information in the header or footer, and title it "References for <your name>." List each reference with contact information, and a brief one-sentence description of how you know or have worked with each person. Examples of suitable descriptions include:

- Served on the Board of the AMA chapter together from 2014–2016
- Direct supervisor at XYZ Corporation; can attest to my team work skills and attention to detail

- Ad agency account executive; worked together on the XYZ account
- Youth Ministry Pastor of XYZ church; worked together to host the summer Vacation Bible Camp in 2015
- Professor of Marketing for 3 courses from 2015–2016; can speak to my work ethic and dedication to my passion for marketing
- Customer from 2010–2013; provided accounting services to his family-run landscaping business Business executive, longtime family friend; familiar with personal background and values

Take several copies of this list of references to your job interview. If the company seems interested, leave one copy with the HR director. Keep one handy to use in filling out the Job Application, which they will probably ask you to complete, even though they have your detailed resume.

Save the file in both Word and PDF format, so you can forward it to your HR contact with a follow-up email to thank them for your interview.

TIP—Shortcut to Filling Out the Job Application Form

Even through you may have already filled out an online application, HR will undoubtedly ask you to fill out a long and tedious hard copy application form during an in-person interview. What they really need is your signature giving them the legal right to contact former employers for references and to perform credit and criminal background searches. So shortcut the application by filling out just the contact information, Social Security number (make sure you have it memorized), anything that's NOT on your resume or list of references, and signing and dating the application. Write in pen *"See attached résumé"* on all sections covered by your résumé. Then attach your resume and list of references to the application with a paperclip (which you will bring in your briefcase) and hand it in to HR. It will look much better than trying to hand-write lots of information into too-tiny spaces, and your application will be clean and neat. Five minutes and you're done!

Let Each Reference Know to Expect a Call—And Coach Them On a Suggested Response

After sharing the list of references with a prospective employer, call each listed reference and let them know that they may receive a call asking for a reference. Tell them something like, *"I just applied for a job at XYZ corporation working in social media marketing for their automobile insurance division, and I listed you as a ref-*

erence. Hopefully, you will get a phone call. If you do hear from them, I'd really appreciate it if you mentioned what a good job we did together on the Jones account last year and how we grew sales by 27%."

You don't want them to just say, *"Yeah, she worked for me—I don't remember when."* You can benefit from reminding them of dates, stats accomplishments, and specifics that they can mention so their talking points will be fresh on their mind.

Lastly, ask them to give you a quick call if they DO get contacted by HR to let you know specific questions they asked, if they appeared to have any concerns or interest, and what your reference said about you. It will help you gauge how likely you are to get an offer.

TIP—Understand What Former Employers May and May Not Say About You

In today's litigious society, employers are hesitant to say too much or too little about you for fear of being sued. Each state has a different law about what can and cannot be disclosed in response to a request for employment verification, from almost nothing to a great deal of information—some of which you may not want revealed. If a prospective employer calls an HR department, the information they will receive is limited. The most they might receive is confirmation of:

- Whether or not you were ever employed by the company

- Your title or position
- Your dates of employment
- Your compensation level—confirmation of what you stated you earned
- Whether or not you are eligible to be rehired—it's the legal way to find out if you were fired or left in bad standing

---

TAKEAWAY—Your list of references is very important because it gets beyond the barrier of the HR department to put a prospective employer in touch with someone who will give you a rave review.

TO DO LIST:

- Make a list of professional and personal references and have on hand at or after an interview.
- Include name, current contact information, and info on how you worked together in the past.
- Call or email to get permission to use each as a reference before finalizing the list.

- Call each reference when you expect a company to check your references to coach them on dates and key projects and achievements.

EXAMPLE

IRA N. NIHANT

1555 55th Avenue South-East, Apartment 5, Cloud City, MT 59001
Email: *XXXXXX@stcloudstate.edu | **Phone**: (980) 555-5555*

References:

Ms. Kris Krista
Senior Manager of Information Technology and Marketing
Maverick Software Consulting – Montana State University
ISELF 205
720 4th Avenue South, Cloud City, MT 59001
Phone: (406) 555-5555

Relationship: Ms. Krista is my current manager. Please speak to Ms. Krista regarding my technological background, team development and work ethic within the technological environment.

Ms. Sandy Sandra
Coordinator of Technology Department
HuskyTech - Montana State University
720 4th Avenue South, Cloud City, MT 59001
Phone: (406) 555-5555

Relationship: Ms. Sandra was my manager within the Tech department at HuskyTech. Please speak to Ms. Sandra regarding team work, work ethic, customer service, management and technological document maintenance.

Mr. Tom Thomas
Accountant of HuskyTech
720 4th Avenue South, Cloud City, MT 59001
Phone: (406) 555-5555

Relationship: Mr. Thomas was my manager within the Inventory and Purchasing department at HuskyTech. Please refer to him for inventory management, customer service, team work and work ethic.

FIGURE 12.1 Reference page example.

Assignment: Develop a Reference Sheet

An effective reference sheet includes 3–5 people who will speak well about you and your performance. Identify 3–5 people who would act as references for you. Create a reference sheet. Use appropriate header formatting, including your name and contact information. Use the CRAP design elements discussed earlier in the chapter to effectively format your reference page.

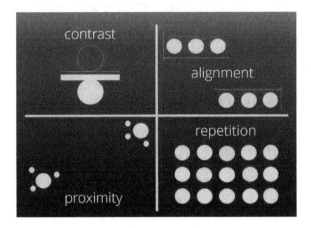

FIGURE 12.2 CRAP elements.

Reading 12.3

Resumes and Portfolios for New Graduates

How to Showcase Potential

By Michelle A. Riklan

Today's Traditional Resume

Resume writers and career coaches can apply a variety of techniques and strategies to create relevant and effective resumes for fresh graduates.

Tie action verbs with numbers and statistics of the applicant's work performance. Many fresh graduates have worked in a retail or food business during at least one point in their college lives. It may be the only job experience that some graduates have. Unfortunately, job descriptions for retail and service jobs don't always translate well into the applicant's target industry.

What resume writers can do is translate unrelated job experience into relatable tasks and quantified information. Figures and specifics are more impressive than standard job descriptions for roles such as retail clerk or fast-food counter person. And even when specific performance results are not available, the numbers speak for themselves to verify the candidate's experiences and abilities.

Example for a store clerk: Part of five-person team that generated more than $30,000 in average daily sales.

Example for a fast-food associate: Worked in a fast-paced customer-service role assisting more than 1,000 customers each day.

Focus on the skills employers want. According to the previously referenced CareerBuilder survey, employers hire candidates who have the ability to communicate clearly, solve difficult problems, and think well under pressure. As career professionals, we need to find a way to translate our clients' skills and college education into those sought-after attributes.

According to Jaime S. Fall, Vice President of HR Policy Association, *"[fresh graduates]are very good at finding information, but not as good at putting that information into context."* He agrees that this generation is very good with technology, but adds that they're not that good in applying those skills in the real world of business.

We can help fresh graduates disprove this common belief by adding to their resumes a variety of accomplishments from undergraduate work experience, volunteer work, and extra-curricular activities. Try to emphasize situations where research skills and technological savvy were used to solve conflicts and demonstrate the ability to make logical decisions based on presented facts.

Example: Created an online check-out system for the Architecture Library, allowing users to process their own returns and saving more than four hours of staff time each week.

Example: Identified five potential new product lines to help local retailer attract more business from college students. Performed detailed marketing, sales, and profit analysis of each product and assisted owner in introducing two promising lines. Both products outperformed projections by at least 10 per cent in first six months.

Check to be sure the resume is well-written and easy to understand. Employers want candidates who can communicate well. The resume is where the employer will first check the candidate's communication skills, so it should be flawless.

The resume should also be written in the language and technical jargon of the job applicant's target industry, but it shouldn't read like a science or technology journal. Relevant certifications, memberships, and technical skills should be included to demonstrate the applicant's familiarity with the job and industry, but the resume should be easily understand by the average (non-technical) reader.

Highlight extra-curricular, volunteer, and other activities relevant to the position. If the applicant hasn't held a single internship or job before graduating from college, including the "extras" is one of the best ways to showcase his experience to potential employers.

Participation in clubs, volunteer efforts, and professional organizations shows dedication, responsibility, and willingness to learn. An affiliation with professional organizations related to the target job also counts as a plus to the job applicant's credentials and work experience, especially if he's done anything to improve the organization.

This is certainly an area where a professional resume writer or career coach can assist the graduate. Often, fresh graduates do not realize that their contributions had value. But experiences such as managing events, helping with fund-raisers, performing marketing activities, leading teams, engaging volunteers, communicating with school administrators, representing the organization to the press, and other activities can demonstrate a wide range of valuable skills.

These activities, when well positioned, will elevate the resume of a fresh graduate from *total newbie* to *valuable intern* or *potential asset* in the eyes of recruiters. Take a look:

Example of fund-raising leadership: Chaired annual fund-raising event that generated more than $10K in support of arts enrichment program in local schools. Led a team of seven volunteers and managed all marketing, publicity, social media, and media relations.

Example of extra-curricular activity: Helped start the school's first table tennis club. Built awareness through public speaking and social media outreach. Negotiated with school administrators for use of facility and purchase of equipment. Published monthly newsletter. Set up tournaments and secured prize donations from local merchants. Attracted 30 players weekly and 80+ for year-end tournament.

The Rise of Unconventional Resumes

The traditional resume is still an effective and expected part of the application process. But in a competitive employment market, all job applicants—and especially fresh graduates—need to consider unconventional and creative approaches to capture attention. By extension, career professionals need to get creative, too. We need to stay on top of changing trends and be prepared to create additional documents to help graduates make a stronger case for their credentials.

Portfolios—The 21st Century Resume

Four out of five employers agree that electronic portfolios can increase the chances for an applicant's resume to get noticed. Why do fresh graduates need a portfolio when they haven't had actual professional work? Portfolios are a big deal, especially for creative and design work, because they are the physical manifestation of the applicant's creativity, technical knowledge, and professional skills. A portfolio provides supporting evidence of a candidate's skills, knowledge, GPA, coursework, and all the claims in her resume.

Writers and media practitioners can assemble a portfolio in the form of websites, clips, and press releases submitted to other publications. Published work is proof that the applicant does have the communication skills, research abilities, and technical know-how to work in the media and communications business.

For graduates of computer sciences and programming, their portfolio may come in the form of written programs, codes, and apps. Their digital portfolio could be their website or their app store.

For some industries, the portfolio might not be a literal portfolio or collection of completed works. Instead, it could be a collection of achievements, awards, journals published, studies, and distinctions.

The portfolio can be included in the traditional resume in a number of ways: URLs (live links) or scannable QR codes can be embedded in the resume, allowing an instantaneous link to the candidate's digital portfolio. In addition, details of the portfolio can be mentioned in the resume through listings of projects, programs, publications, and other distinctions.

Video Resumes—An Enhancement to the Traditional Resume

Please note, video resumes can't and shouldn't replace formal resumes and should not be used to tell the applicant's entire story. That would make the video resume too long and probably not very interesting! But a video resume can be a good supplement to a traditional resume and a way for the applicant to reveal personality as well as talents and skills.

A video resume should be short, ideally no longer than five minutes. Its purpose is to showcase the applicant's communication skills in a way that's not possible with a text-only resume. Aside from that, it could also be used to share creative materials, pitch a quick idea, and showcase the applicant's research skills by demonstrating knowledge of the company.

Career professionals can help their clients create compelling video resumes by evaluating what to present in the video, writing or editing the script, and coaching on presentation.

Each Resume Gets Only 5–7 Seconds

A recent survey from The Ladders (2012) reveals that recruiters spend an average of six seconds reviewing a resume, while another study from BeHiring (as quoted by Dr. John Sullivan on ere.net, 2013) says the time is five to seven seconds.

Considering this, the challenge faced by fresh graduates who don't have much experience rises. Of course, career professionals face the same pressure—How can we give fresh graduates a fighting chance when we have only six seconds to make an impression on their behalf? The answer lies in the numbers. According to TheLadders survey, about four seconds of

the six-second interval is focused on four key areas of the resume:

Job titles
Previous companies
Start and end dates of employment
Education

The best approach, then, is to use Parts 1–3 of the resume (as listed above) to highlight internships, volunteer activities, related projects, and portfolio—all of the things that fresh graduates have to offer, written in language the potential employer can relate to.

References

Chronicle of Higher Education and American Public Media's Marketplace. The Role of Higher Education in Career Development: Employer Perceptions (2012). http://chronicle.com/items/biz/pdf/Employers%20 Survey.pdf

More Employers Finding Reasons Not to Hire Candidates on Social Media, Finds CareerBuilder Survey (2013). CareerBuilder.com. http:// cb.com/18kvlj1 http://www.hrpolicy.org/

Sullivan, John. Why You Can't Get a Job ... Recruiting Explained by the Numbers (2013). Ere.net. http://www.ere.net/2013/05/20/why-you-can'tget-a-job-recruiting-explained-by-the-numbers/

TheLadders.com. You have Six Seconds to Make an Impression: How Recruiters See Your Resume (2012). http://info.theladders.com/our-team/ you-only-get-6-seconds-of-fame-make-it-count

About the Author

Michelle A. Riklan, ACRW, CPRW, CEIC, is a frequent media guest, professional resume writer, career coach, training/workshop facilitator, author, and speaker. With a combined 25 years of in-house corporate and targeted consulting experience, she services large corporations as well as small businesses and individuals in all aspects of organizational development, career management, and outplacement. She is the producer of the National Career Summit, a virtual online event that brought together some of the most respected names in business, leadership, and career coaching. She is co-author / contributor to multiple published career books including *101 Great Ways to Enhance Your Career* and *101 Great Ways to Compete in Today's Job Market*.

Contact her as follows: *michelle@riklanresources.com*

Assignment: Write a Resume

Write a resume targeted at the ad you identified earlier. Bring the rough resume to class for peer review and activities. Then, following feedback, edit your resume, incorporating changes you think are most effective for your situation.

Applying This Skill: Student Resume Analysis: Find the Error

In your small group, review the resumes on the following pages. Order the resumes from best to worst and create a list of reasons for your decision. Indicate any changes you would make on the best resume(s).

Bonus: Several semesters ago, students turned in these resumes. I was disappointed with all the students' work. On the best resume, I found an error that made me return all the resumes without grading them. Can you find the error that made me return all the resumes?

RESUME ANALYIS EXAMPLE 1
Rate   1   2   3   4   5

ERIC DONNAL
500 first Ave. S, Lawrence Hall #333
Saint Cloud , MN, 56301
edxxxl @stcloudstate.ed u
651-555-5555

EDUCATION:

Saint Cloud State University, St Cloud, M N   Expected May 2018
- Third year student
- International Business
- GPA 3.69

EXPERIENCE:

St. Cloud State University, St. Cloud, M N
- Community Advisor, residential life   August 2015- May 2016
                                                         August 2016 -May 2017
- Conference Crew Manager   May 2016 –August 2016

Volunteer-
- Volunteered to cook in Anna Maries   Feb 9, 2015
- Volunteered to teach Basic English Language in Jalim Bihani Primary School
  and Arunodaya Academy for the primary level students, in Nepal.
                                                         June 2013- Aug 2013

AFFILIATIONS AND ACTIVITIES
- College Senator position for Student Government   Aug 2016 – May 2017
- Public relation officer for the club Student Organized for Change (SOC Club).
                                                                October 2015
- Member of Nepalese Student Association (NSA).   August 2014 - present

ADDITIONAL SKILLS
- Communication, Counseling/ Advising, Customer Service, Dependable,
  Teaching/Training, Working in Teams
- **Computer Skills:** Software packages- MS PowerPoi nt, MS Word, MS Excel.
- **Language Skills:** Fluent in English, Nepali and Hindi.

ACTIVITIES AND ACHIEVEMENTS
- Got into **Dean's list** du ring the first semester and forth semester of college
                                                   December 2014, May 2016
- Got acknowledged by Residential Life for **Academic Achievement** during my
  first semester.   December 2014

RESUME ANALYIS EXAMPLE 2

Rate   1   2   3   4   5

Claire Smith

4555 Pleasant Ave NW, Annandale, MN I 320-555-5556 Icsxxxx@stcloudstate.edu

Education

St Cloud State University
Accounting Major
GPA: 3.26

Work Experience

French Lake Curb Company
Bookkeeper/Laborer   May 2015-Present
- Payroll/ pay payroll taxes
- File taxes (941, Unemployment)
- Bank Reconciliations
- Laborer working on the crew as well as bookkeeping

Clarke Environmental   May 2013- August, 2014
Field Technician
- Sprayed yards and towns for mosquitoes
- Ensured quality personalized service for each client

Additional Leadership & Volunteer Experience

- Volunteer Annandale/Maple Lake Youth Wrestling Coach   November 2011- March 2013

Additional Professional Skills

- Proficient in Microsoft Office including Excel, Word, and PowerPoint
- QuickBooks accounting software
- Skilled with computers

References

Available upon request

RESUME ANALYIS EXAMPLE 3

Rate   1   2   3   4   5

MARIE R. ANDERSON

5555 5 Ave • International Falls, MN 56649 • (555) 455-555 • maXXXX@STCLOUDSTATE.EDU

EDUCATION

BACHELOR'S OF SCIENCE IN FINANCE   Anticipated Graduation May 2017
Saint Cloud State University (SCSU), Saint Cloud, Minnesota
- Program nationally accredited by the Association to Advance Collegiate Schools of Business (AACSB)
- Recipient of Presidential Academic Scholarship
- Working over 24 hours bi-weekly while attending college full-time.
- 3.57 Cumulated GPA

STUDY ABROAD EXPERIENCE

PROPERTY SALES & COMMUNITY RELATIONS INTERN   January 2016- May 2016
First National Real Estate, Mosman, NSW Australia

- Compare a property with similar properties that have recently sold to determine its competitive market place
- Promote sales of properties through advertisements, open houses, and participation in multiple listing services
- Develop and maintain a database stored procedures, views and functions for hosted web applications

EMPLOYMENT

BUSINESS ADVISING DESK RECEPTIONIST   March 2015-Present
St. Cloud State University, Saint Cloud, Minnesota
- Provide assistance to students to meet with an advisor

- Arrange records to increase functionality of the working environment and confidentiality of student files
- Manage office operations, including mail and a staff of five with a result to increase productivity

SERVER/BARTENDER   May 2016-Present
Cha Cha Resort, International Falls, Minnesota
- Identify customers' needs and problem-solve accordingly, using quick-thinking and strong judgment
- Display both excellent work ethic and customer-focus during high-traffic shifts

- Demonstrate a positive attitude is high pressure situations to increase colleague morale and improve teamwork, resulting in stronger customer service overall

SERVER   May 2014-July 2015
Bond's Resort, Baudette, Minnesota

- Developed strong interpersonal communication skills by providing quality service to thousands of restaurant customers
- Accepted credit card payments and worked with P.O.S registers to accurately secure payment and funds
- Learned how to multi-task and handle pressure of a fast-paced work environment in a professional manner

EXTRACARRICULAR EXPERIENCE

PEER EDUCATOR   August 2015-Present
Orientation to the Herberger Business School
- Accurately take attendance, update grade book regularly, and answer students questions in class
- Tutor and mentor students utilizing strong leadership skills

ADMINISTRATIVE OFFICER / SOCIAL COORDINATOR   August 2016-Present
Herberger Business School Investment Club
- Plan social gatherings for group members to get to know one and other better
- Send emails regarding what our meetings concluded to keep members updated

ADDITIONAL SKILLS

- Experience with Microsoft Office - Word, PowerPoint & Excel
- Excellent communication skills with an emphasis on customer service
- Proficient in organizing and planning

RESUME ANALYIS EXAMPLE 4

Rate 1 2 3 4 5

JOHN JOHNSON

1900 Maple Road, Saint Cloud, MN 56303 • (320)555-5555 • jjXXXXX@stcloudstate.edu

PROFESSIONAL OBJECTIVE

Seeking a Tax Accountant Internship for spring 2018

EDUCATION

Saint Cloud State University - Saint Cloud, MN
Accredited by Association to Advance Collegiate Schools of Business
Bachelor of Arts in Accounting
Expected Graduation: Summer 2018 with 150 credit hours
GPA: 3.92
Worked 25 hours per week while attending college full-time

EXPERIENCE

Accounting Clerk/Receptionist/Cashier
Eich Motor Company - Saint Cloud, MN   June 2014 - Current
- Journalizing, posting, and creating adjusting entries in ADP
- Met deadlines preparing and organizing monthly parts statements and audit trails for accounting purposes
- Manage opening and closing duties as assigned and provide quality service to hundreds of customers
- Display strong attention to detail, managing money transactions and daily receipts
- Work well as a member of a team, helping to maintain a positive attitude among team members
- Learn and use skills in efficiently executing cash transactions by operating own cash register
- Demonstrate ability to effectively multi-task in a fast-paced work environment

Independent Contractor
Saint Cloud Times - Saint Cloud, MN   October 2010 - January 2015
- Successfully controlled two Shopping News routes in a dependable and dedicated manner

VOLUNTEERING & SERVICE

Saint Michael's Church - Saint Cloud, MN   December 2008 - Current
- Leader of Vacation Bible School from 2010-2013
- Bring the Church Community together by providing refreshments after Mass

Saint Cloud State University - Saint Cloud, MN   September 2015 - May 2016
- Note taker for Student Disability Services
- Tutor for Accounting

AFFILIATIONS & ACTIVITIES

Beta Gamma Sigma - International Business Honor Society   April 2016 - Current
- Membership based on high scholastic achievement

Saint Cloud State Accounting Club - Saint Cloud, MN   August 2015 - Current
- Social Coordinator and set up annual Golf Outing

SKILLS

- Client-focused
- Detail oriented
- Microsoft Office, Excel, PowerPoint proficiency

- Quick learner
- Cooperative team member
- Specialized automotive accounting knowledge

AWARDS & HONORS

James W. Miller Family Scholarship
Saint Cloud State University - August 2014

Presidential Academic Scholarship
Saint Cloud State University - August 2014

- Rewarded for academic achievement & service
- Received based on ACT score of 28

RESUME ANALYIS EXAMPLE 5
Rate   1   2   3   4   5

Kris Manson

- Permanent Address: 7555 County Road 15, Bird Island, MN   55310
- Cell Number : 320-555-555
- E-mail: kxxxxxxx@gmail.com

OBJECTIVE

I am a full time student interested in gaining "hands-on" experience though an internship position. Graduating spring 2017.

EDUCATION

St. Cloud State University,   2014 - Present
St. Cloud, MN

- Major in Communication Studies with an emphasis in Organizational   Leadership.
- Minor in Business Marketing.
- British Studies - Education Abroad Program Spring 2016.

WORK EXPERIENCE

St. Cloud State Athletics Department September 2016- Present
St. Cloud, MN

Position: Marketing Specialist

Minnesota Viking's LLC June 2016 - Present
Eden Prairie, MN

Position: Public Relations part time intern:
- Training Camp summer 2016
- Game Day 2016-2017 Season.

Bernick's Pepsi June 2016 - Present
St. Cloud, MN

Position: Brand Ambassador

Harvest land Cooperative   May -August 2015
Morgan, MN

Position: Marketing and Communications Intern

REFERENCES

Available upon request

Applying This Skill: Student Resume Analysis: Peer Review Best Resume Exercise

In your small group, gather all rough draft resumes into a pile. When instructed, pass the pile to another group. When you receive a new group of resumes, determine which one you like the most. List the specific design features and content elements that make this resume effective but not any suggestions for further improvement. Be prepared to share your document and findings with the class.

Applying This Skill: Peer Review Resume

Swap resumes with a classmate. Using the checklist below, review your partner's resume. Discuss areas of success and areas that need improvement.

Assess Your Document Here

Resume Format & Checklist

Complete header
□————→

Samantha Smith
Address, email, phone, LinkedIn profile address

Section Heading
□————→ **Education**

List, degree, school
□————→

Bachelor of Science, Accounting   Expected May 2018
St. Cloud State University (SCSU), St. Cloud, MN
Accredited by Association to Advance Collegiate Schools   □
of Business—International   Align dates

List other relevant info   Format dates
□————→
- Work 30 hours/wk
- GPA 3.3
- 50 credits

Section Heading
□————→ **Experience**

Position & Company
□————→

Intern   Dec 2017-Apr 2018
JCWM Company, Becker, MN

List skills developed
Quantify if possible
□————→
- Reviewed clients' accounting and operating procedures
- Audited a variety of areas of financial statements and note disclosures
- Prepared 3 small audits

Section Heading
□————→ **Volunteer Experience**

Position & Company
□————→

Volunteer   Dec 2015-present
Hands Across the World, St. Cloud, MN

List skills developed
□————→
- Demonstrated effective communication and leadership skills while working with 2-5 immigrants per session
- Taught English, mathematics, computer skills

Section Heading
□————→ **Activities and Achievements**

Co-President, The Accounting Club of SCSU   Jan 2017-present
Member, The International Honor Society Beta
Gamma Signma   March 2015-present
Recipient, Dean's List   Dec 2016, May 2017
Recipient, Johnson Memorial Scholarship   2014

□————→ **Additional Skills**

□————→

Spanish, French
Proficient in CCH Prosystem Engagement, QuickBooks

□ Use of design elements
□ No errors in spelling

FIGURE 12.9 Resume checklist and check list.

Applying This Skill: Partner Bullet Point Development

Partner with a classmate. Look at your partner's resume and select 2–3 bullet points to ask about. Say something like: "Tell me more about what you did here" or "Tell me more about this." As your partner talks, take notes about what s/he is saying. This will help identify words, skills, accomplishments, etc. your partner may use to strengthen the bullet points.

Bullet Point: _____

Notes:

Bullet Point: _____

Notes:

Bullet Point: _____

Notes:

13   Cover/Job Application Letters

Whenever you submit a resume, you should include a cover letter. Sometimes they will be printed, like a resume, but most online application sites have a place for you to insert or upload your cover letter with your resume. If there is an option to include a cover letter, you need to do so. If you are emailing a resume, you may attach a cover letter to the email. If your resume makes it through the first round of review, then a recruiter or hiring manager will read your cover letter. The cover letter is how you introduce yourself; it presents your personality, your uniqueness, and your interest in or passion for the position. An effective cover letter will help you make the best impression you can. After completing this lesson, you will:

- Understand how to and demonstrate your ability to create an effective cover letter
- Understand the importance of and how to target your job application documents

Reading 13.1

Transforming Generic Resumes and Cover Letters to Laser-Focused Career Communications

By Laura Gonzalez

The Cover Letter

Job seekers may find generic cover letters even more tempting to use than generic resumes. But a generic cover letter is no more useful than a generic resume. An astute hiring manager can identify a cover letter that is meant only to meet the minimum requirement of sending a cover letter, while not actually providing unique and relevant information. Cover letters that are written to be applicable to every opportunity, company, and profession usually sound vague and unappealing, especially if there is nothing that connects the prospective employee to the job, the company, or the industry.

Generic cover letters say quite a lot about a prospective employee. When reading the document, the hiring manager may assume that the job seeker is:

- Dispassionate about wanting to work for the company.
- In too much of a hurry to spend a few minutes personalizing the letter.
- Too busy to follow instructions or procedures properly.
- Only willing to put partial effort into important tasks.

Not very positive positioning, is it?

Specific Cover Letters Work

A proper cover letter must be focused on the open position and must provide specific details that paint a picture of what the job seeker brings to that job and that company. A cover letter allows the job seeker many advantages that a resume alone does not—opportunities to include information not appropriate for a resume; opportunities to share career stories; opportunities to mention network contacts or industry knowledge; and much more. As such, a job seeker should always include a cover letter unless the application instructions expressly forbid one.

A job seeker's cover letter can:

- Complement a resume and overcome its inherent restrictions.
- Explain any potential questions regarding the resume.
- Overcome issues that might eliminate the job seeker from the prospect pool.
- Begin building a relationship with the hiring manager.
- Connect skills, experience, and achievements to the needs of the hiring manager.

The cover letter can complement a resume and overcome its inherent restrictions. The cover letter allows the job seeker to show personality, to emphasize a relevant piece of information from the resume, and to add additional information that does not fit in the resume. The cover letter is a great opportunity to persuade the employer that the job seeker is worth the effort of an interview.

The cover letter is the place to share a job seeker's career story, mention network contacts or references, highlight industry knowledge, and much more. A well-written cover letter gives tremendous power to the job seeker to make things happen: specifically, to generate an interview.

The cover letter can explain potential questions regarding a resume. The cover letter allows the job seeker to provide explanations for the things that will either be red flags or questions for the hiring manager. If the job seeker knows that he has an issue that will be quickly picked up in the resume, then the cover letter is his first (and sometimes only) opportunity to explain that issue. For example, if there are gaps in employment or if the job seeker experienced a career transition, the cover letter can provide a detailed explanation in just a few brief sentences.

Read through the excerpt below for one such possibility:

After designing and selling a successful product line to JCPenny (iBaby brand clothing) and raising my daughter for the past 5 years, I am now ready to rejoin the clothing industry in a marketing manager role. My sabbatical allowed me to discover an interesting opportunity—a new way to combine consumer goods with technology trends. This knowledge can be paired with my extensive experience to make an immediately positive impact for (name of company).

In every case, the job seeker must tailor the cover letter to the opportunity, using the document to demonstrate that she has what it takes to do the job. It is important for the job seeker to provide examples of skills and achievements that show she will be a positive force in the company's work environment. The example below shows how the job seeker uses achievements from previous positions to show how she is a great fit for the new role.

In each of my past positions, I have earned the title of *Revitalization Expert*. My management roles were filled with the same kinds of challenges your company is currently facing, including budget management issues and unmotivated teams. Let me show you how I solved these problems for my previous employers:

- When I first joined RoyalMix Inc., I was tasked to complete a major project—without enough money to do so! The budget had been erroneously assigned (discovered late into the project). I held a cross-team brainstorming session to find small ways to save money. I ensured the project was completed to the specifications of both the company and the client, which later led to additional contracts for my employer.
- My current position provided me with ample opportunities to turn around my teams. I led six teams that felt unmotivated and overworked during the company's merger. I personally sat down with each team member to learn more about their issues. I then implemented a new reward system and scheduled regular meetings to get them back on track. Several of my teams earned prestigious productivity awards after that change!

The cover letter can overcome issues that the employer will use to eliminate job seekers from the prospective pool. For example, if a job seeker lacks experience in a certain area, the cover letter can be used to explain how seemingly unrelated experience and abilities transfer and make up for the lack. If the job seeker has skills that are appropriate to the company, but not the specific job, he can tell the reader about those skills. Employers are planning years in the future, and if the job seeker is fluent in a language that will be needed when the organization expands its operations, that skill is positive information that solidifies a job seeker's potential worth to the company.

The example below demonstrates how a new graduate used her academics in place of work experience:

> During my time at the University of Pennsylvania, I scheduled myself for every possible course in advertising. I wanted to see how an advertising campaign can combine different styles and media to convey one idea. This interest inspired my final capstone project: a viral advertising campaign for Sephora's new makeup line. I created several advertising pieces:
>
> - YouTube series of makeovers with the new products, inspiring several key YouTube makeup casters to host competitions.
> - Facebook campaign and three-part contest to cover each major product area.
> - In-store product placement and new advertising design to lead customers directly to the new products.
>
> My professor was so impressed with my work that he informed his Sephora contact of my campaign. This led to an advertising internship to implement a social media strategy. I was complimented by upper management several times for my innovative approaches.

The cover letter is a fantastic first opportunity to build a relationship with the hiring manager. One way to demonstrate expertise in the cover letter is to speak the language of the hiring manager by using common terminology for the position. It is important, however, to avoid using acronyms that are company-specific or industry-specific since the words may not mean anything outside the job seeker's original organization.

The job seeker's goal is to explain what she can achieve for the hiring manager in the new position, while also clearly demonstrating overall industry knowledge. For example, take a look at the sentence below:

"In my previous position I handled ADQs and MDLs successfully, meeting my quota and never resorting to GLMOGRE that my colleagues used."

While ADQ and MDL may be industry terminology, GLMOGRE may mean nothing to a hiring manager if it was specific to the past position and prior company. It is much better to translate the company jargon into words and phrases that will transfer to the new company.

This is also an important consideration in case the cover letter ends up in the hands of a HR person who may not be familiar with the jargon. For example:

"In my previous position I ensured data accuracy, managed monthly financial reporting, and exceeded performance goals."

This second sentence is much more descriptive of what the job seeker has done in the past and what he proposes to do for the hiring manager in the future, without utilizing jargon that has no meaning to the new position or company.

But there is also a middle ground the job seeker can take. Very common terminology—such as PDF, B2B, B2C, P&L, and other abbreviations and acronyms—are generally acceptable and understandable for anyone reading the cover letter (depending on the industry). The job seeker should take time to read through the job description and the company's information before deciding what industry jargon to include and what to leave out.

The cover letter can make the connection between past experience and knowledge and the position that is being filled. In fact, every sentence and piece of information that is included in the cover letter should contribute toward the job seeker's suitability for the position. The job seeker can use the questions below to double-check the relevance of the information in the cover letter:

- Why is this information included in the letter?
- What does this information suggest you can do for the hiring manager?
- How does this information show what you can do for the employer?
- Is the information descriptive and detailed?
- Have you provided additional information in the letter that was not in the resume?

- If the information is repeated from the resume, have you appropriately reworded it so that it is not simply copied and pasted?

The cover letter should focus on the company and on the position; it should demonstrate exactly what the job seeker can accomplish based on past experience and accomplishments. The job seeker should take time to analyze her skills, knowledge, and experience and then create content to demonstrate concretely how these areas relate to the position. The details should take the form of linear, easy-to-understand connections that follow what the job seeker has done, what she knows, what she has accomplished, and how these things directly apply to the desired position. The job seeker should not waste space with information, facts, and details that do not matter to the prospective employer.

As an example, take a look at the two sentences below. The first, while filled with great imagery, needs to be better tied to the goal. The second sentence is more to the point, but could be too short to catch the reader's attention.

"As I wandered around the gorgeous museums of Madrid, Spain, I pondered how I could translate my love of Iberian art into a fulfilling career that would challenge me and sustain my goal of becoming the youngest Vice President of Marketing of a Fortune 500 company in history."

"As a recent graduate, I believe my art history courses and recent tour of museums in Madrid, Spain, would allow me to write effective copy for your art auction catalogs."

The key here is to strike a balance between the two sentences. It is important to show passion in the cover letter, especially in the introduction, so that the reader will be intrigued enough to continue looking through the document. But it is equally important to be concise and always target the position. If the first job seeker edited down the imagery and firmly explained why it tied into the goal, and the second job seeker expanded on why she is a dedicated, hard-working graduate with fantastic potential skills, then both job seekers could be successful. It's all about balance!

Cover Letter Presentation

Cover letters, in Word and pdf, should have a clean format that matches the resume. Letters pasted directly into the email message won't match precisely, but use the same font when you can for consistency in presentation.

Whenever possible, the job seeker should research the hiring manager's name and position and use it in the cover letter. If not, he can opt for no salutation at all or use *Dear Hiring Manager* (my least favorite option).

It is critical to edit and proofread diligently. The job seeker should check and recheck spelling, details (such as the position title and company name), and contact information in the address to make sure that everything is correct. It is not uncommon for a hiring manager to move on to the next candidate based on careless editing of the cover letter.

Conclusion

Generic documents cause more problems than they solve. A job seeker's cover letter and resume should both be well-written and laser-focused to each position to achieve the best results. Targeted documents will help the job seeker capture and hold the reader's attention while getting across the requisite skills, experience, and achievements. As with many other endeavors, preparation is the key to success in any job search and in lifelong career management.

About the Author

Laura Gonzalez, ACRW, CPRW, is a twice-certified expert resume writer who has led 6,000+ clients to excel in the job hunt by crafting modern and targeted resumes, cover letters, CVs, LinkedIn profiles, and more. She specializes in identifying, strengthening, and positioning key achievements on documents to capture and hold the reader's attention. She works with clients at any career level (student/entry-level through C-level and beyond) in nearly every industry imaginable. Laura's documents have also earned industry recognition; she received an award nomination for one of her senior-level resumes.

Prior to launching her business full time, she worked for years at the University of Texas at Dallas Career Center as a resume expert. She created numerous handouts and documents for students, alumni, and faculty that are still in use today. She also presented more than 50 seminars on a variety of career topics: resumes, cover letters, LinkedIn profiles and social media, career expos, and much more. Her academic background is now frequently utilized for new graduates needing strong documents to get ahead in the job search.

Contact her as follows:
laura@masterworkresumes.com

Assess Your Document Here   **Job Application Letter Format & Checklist**

☐⟶   **Samantha Smith**
                Use Same Header as on Resume and Reference Sheet

☐⟶   Date here

☐⟶   Receiver's name
      and address

☐⟶   Salutation here:

☐⟶   Opening Paragraph: Catch reader's attention. Name position applying
      for and where learned of it. Indicate interest in position. Preview order
      of topics discussed in body paragraphs.

☐⟶   Body paragraph 1: State main topic with supporting ideas and
      details. Describe situation/scene and action taken. Relate experience/
      qualifications to position/company.

☐⟶   Body paragraph 2: State main topic #2 (topic sentence) with
      supporting ideas and details. As needed, use sub-headings, bullets,
      in-text citations.

☐⟶   Conclusion: Refer to resume. Refer to or request interview/meeting.
      Express enthusiasm and gratitude. Include contact information.

☐⟶   Complementary close here,

☐⟶   *Signature Here*

☐⟶   Printed Name Here
      Additional Contact Information, if not above

☐⟶   Enclosure: Resume
      (indicates to reader that resume is enclosed)

FIGURE 13.1 Cover letter sample & checklist.

Cover Letter

Using the Adapted STAR Method

Format

Includes your contact information

1023 11th Ave S
St. Cloud, MN 56301

April 11, 2014

Bayview Event Center
688 Excelsior Street
Excelsior, MN 55331

Addressed to a person

Dear Ms. Johnson:

The Adapted STAR Method

Situation: give an example of a situation in you were in that resulted in a positive outcome

Task: describe the tasks & challenges involved in the situation

Action: give an example of the actions you took

Results & Relate: describe the results and relate to the position

Show the interviewer how you fit the job

Introduction

Establishes interest by introducing self

Names position & company

The combination of my education, teamwork and communication skills and out-going personality make me an excellent candidate for a customer service in marketing position with the Bayview Event Center. I enjoy making others happy and taking the extra step to ensure they are getting what they want and desire. I am excited about applying my skills in a role as a group sales associate, which was posted on the St. Cloud State University Career Services website.

Indicates where learned of the position

Use networking if applicable

The Conclusion

After you review the attached resume for more information about my work and volunteer experience, please call me at (555) 555-5555 or email me at student@stcloudstate.edu so we may discuss how I can contribute to your company's needs. Thank you for your consideration and I look forward to speaking with you.

Include contact in & encourage action

Sincerely,

Sign Name

Name

The Body

Follows order of ideas

This fall I will graduate with a Bachelor's degree in marketing. Throughout my time at St. Cloud State University, I have learned about customer relations, professional selling and business management. My thorough education will allow me to immediately apply marketing skills as a sales associate with Bayview Event Center.

The most important skill I developed while in school is teamwork which I developed while playing for the St. Cloud State varsity basketball team. When I joined the team as a transfer student, I was immediately looked to as a leader by both coaches and teammates during the season's ups and downs. My longtime friend and starting point guard tore his MCL in his left knee with six games left in the regular season. I gathered the team and reinforced that if we played for our injured teammate and focused on every possession, we would continue to win. We overcame this difficult hurdle to end the season with only one loss and a trip to the conference championship. It is this determination, optimism and teamwork that I will bring to your team at Bayview.

Situation Action

Relates skills to position

FIGURE 13.2 STARR.

Assignment: Write a Cover Letter

Using the principles discussed in this chapter, write a job application/cover letter. The letter should be targeted to a specific job advertisement. Use standard business letter format as discussed in Chapter 6.

When writing your job application/cover letter, recall the SOAR/STAR method discussed in Chapter 14. Some of the most effective cover letters will tell a story or explain a specific situation using the SOAR/STAR pattern. Then, try to relate the skills/qualifications you discussed back to the job you're applying for. Tell the readers how you will help them, solve their problem or fit the requirements of the position. See the infographic "the Adapted STARR Method" below.

TARGETING JOB APPLICATION DOCUMENTS

Once you have a well-formatted reference sheet and resume and a well-written cover letter, what else can you to do make yourself stand out from the dozens or hundreds of other candidates for your ideal job? The best way to make sure your application is seen by the right people is to target your documents to the specific job and company you are applying to.

Companies, using either computer software (called Applicant Tracking Systems) or human resources staff, scan resumes and cover letters for keywords. Keywords are job qualifications, skills, or credentials needed in the position. Matching keywords or candidates allows companies to narrow the applicant pool quickly.

Using the right keywords in your job application documents may be the difference between your getting an interview or not. To identify the right keywords, read the job ad closely. Use the words in the ad in your resume and cover letter. If the ad says the job requires customer service skills, use the words "customer service skills," not "took care of customers." Common keywords include skills such as managing and leading, computer skills, titles of previous positions, licenses, or certifications. Incorporate as many relevant keywords as possible in your resume and cover letter.

Applying This Skill: Peer Review Cover/Job Application Letter

Work with a peer. Trade rough drafts of your cover letters and follow the steps below to provide feedback and suggestions on each other's cover letters.

1. Circle all "I"s in the letter
2. Underline all of the verbs (action words)
3. Suggest two alternative verbs
4. Assess Formatting:
   - One page only
   - Single spacing
   - Left-justified text (no indentation)
   - Blank line between paragraphs
   - Short, unified paragraphs
   - Margins—top, bottom, sides balanced
   - Use header as in resume/Sender address at top
   - Date after sender address
   - Receiver address after date
   - Professional salutation (such as: Ms., Dr., etc.)
   - Colon after salutation

5. Introduction:
   - States position applying for
   - Names source where found position
   - Mentions 2 to 3 qualifications (addressed in letter)
   - Uses networking (if applicable)

6. Body (2-3 Paragraphs):
   - In body paragraphs, in margins write:
   - "S" where writer describes situation
   - "TA" where writer describes tasks or action taken
   - "R" where writer discusses result
   - "RR" where writer related situation/skill to position applying for/ How experience fits position/ company

7. Closing
   - Refers to resume (w/ reason to look)
   - Provides info on how/when to contact
   - Refers to or requests interview (maybe state topics to discuss)
   - Expresses gratitude

Job Ad vs Resume

Ad

HR Recruiter, Internal Temporary

HR RECRUITER MAIN RESPONSIBILITIES

•   Recruit and identify qualified candidates to build and maintain a candidate pool with the goal of eventually interviewing, hiring and placing those who are qualified employees.
•   Manage and develop client relationships. Provide recruiting status updates for open orders, quality checks for employees currently working, and identify potential new orders. Provide updates to Staffing Supervisor or Service Manager on a regular basis.
•   Collaborate with the service team to maximize the level of client service, encourage relationship building, and provide cost effective service solutions to meet customer demands.
•   Work closely with Staffing Manager and Business Development Manager to strategize on methodologies to identify new business opportunities in order to achieve and exceed company financial goals and objectives.
•   Maximize Company's technology to ensure optimum, cost-effective, timely and high quality results.

HR RECRUITER KEY REQUIREMENTS

EDUCATION and/or EXPERIENCE
•   Required: High School Diploma or GED and two years related experience and or training;
•   Preferred: Two years of college and two years related work experience.
•   Must have excellent problem solving and organizational skills.

Resume

Jane Handy
555 Cypress Road, City, State 56303 • (320)555-5559 • jxxxx@emailaddress, JHardyLinkedIn

EDUCATION

College University - City, State   Expected Grad Date
Accredited by AACSB
Bachelor of Science in Management, HR focus
GPA: 3.92
Worked 25 hours per week while attending college full-time

EXPERIENCE
Receptionist/Cashier
Motor Company - City, State   June 2014 -Present
•   Provide quality service to hundreds of customers
•   work well as member of a team, helping to maintain a positive attitude among team members
•   Maximize ability to multi-task in a fast-paced work environment to provide high quality results.

VOLUNTEERING & SERVICE
College University - City, State   September 2015 - May 2016
•   Note taker for Student Disability Services

AFFILIATIONS & ACTIVITIES
Beta Gamma Sigma - International Business Honor Society
•   Membership based on high scholastic achievement
Society for Human Resources Management (SHRM) - City, State
•   Social Coordinator

Match Keywords

FIGURE 13.3 Job Ad Match.

Applying This Skill: Analyzing the Job Ad

Locate an ad for a job you would like to apply for when you graduate. Bring the ad to class. In class, you will complete the following:

1. Read the *entire* ad carefully.
2. Circle competencies/skills/qualifications listed in the ad that you already have.
3. Underline any qualifications/experiences/skills the ad mentions that you are lacking.
4. Fill in the columns below.

At the end of the exercise, you should see which qualifications you have that match the job ad. You will use those matches to enhance your job application. Use as many keywords as possible in your resume and cover letter. In your reference page, list people who will speak about qualifications the job requires. Use the situations/experiences you list to develop SOAR/STAR situations and stories you can use in your cover letter and interviews.

Qualifications I have	Situations/Experiences that demonstrate
Ex: "Ability to build client relationships"	"I interned with Northwestern Mutual and worked with a staff member who showed me how to build a customer base. I developed my ability to contact customers by calling clients, setting up meetings, and following up on contacts. At the end of my internship, I had a client base of ten people."
Qualifications I'm lacking	**How I might develop**
Ex: "Experience with social media recruiting"	"Join AMA and work on social media; get an internship doing social media"

14   Interviewing Skills

Once your resume and cover letter have been reviewed and the company is interested in you, they will call you for an interview. Interviews may take place in an increasing variety of ways, including phone interviews, Skype interviews, panel interviews, and more. No matter what type of interview you face, some basic skills are needed to succeed. In this chapter, you will learn about elevator speeches and behavioral interviewing questions. After completing this lesson, you will:

- Have a prepared and practiced elevator speech
- Be prepared to answer behavioral interviewing questions using the STAR/SOAR method

Reading 14.1

Ace the Interview

By Thea Kelley

The entire interviewing process boils down to one question, whether it is asked in so many words or not: "Why should we hire you (instead of one of our other candidates)?"

This chapter will help you answer that question clearly, credibly, and memorably—not just when it's specifically asked, but throughout your interview process, so that you stand out as "the one."

Relax and Be Confident

Almost everyone is nervous about job interviews. It's normal to have the jitters, or even to be downright scared. But it's not helpful when you're so anxious that you sweat heavily or your mind goes blank.

Relaxation exercises can help you stay calm before and during your interview. Search the Internet for "relaxation techniques Mayo Clinic" and you'll find several exercises you can use anytime, anywhere. Experiment with a few, choose the one you like best, and practice it frequently so it's ready when you need it.

As for confidence, that comes from being prepared. Put in some time and practice, and use everything you learn in this chapter to get thoroughly ready for successful job interviews. If you've been "winging it" until now, you may be amazed at how much more confident you'll feel when you're properly prepared.

Now let's think about the main messages you want to confidently communicate in your interviews.

Communicate Your Key Selling Points

There may be 50 reasons why a certain employer should hire you, but nobody can remember 50 reasons.

So, narrow it down: What's the number one factor that is most likely to make them want to hire you? Now think of a few others that are almost as powerful. Those are your key selling points.

Ask yourself these questions to help you identify your key selling points:

- What qualifications do I have that are hard to find?
- What do I do better than my peers?
- What have my employers appreciated most about me?
- What are the most impressive accomplishments in my resume?

Once you have a short list, review it to make sure your key selling points are:

- **Relevant from the employer's point of view:** Although you might think the best reason to hire you is that you write very creatively, the employer may be more interested in your achievements in configuring databases.
- **Exceptional:** Presumably, all the candidates have the basic skills to do the job. What do you have that's above and beyond or hard to find?

Tell a Story

Stories are to interviews what pictures are to a website. They illustrate the content and make it much more engaging. Stories are often required by the way an interview question is phrased. When you hear "tell me about a time when you (handled this or that)," you're being asked a behavioral interview question, which requires you to tell a story. Having plenty of stories ready is a must.

Even when a story isn't asked for, it can liven up your answer. A well-told story enables the interviewer to imagine you doing skillful work and achieving results. In her mind's eye she can actually see it—and seeing is believing.

You used stories earlier in the book to identify skills and craft accomplishment statements for your resume using the CAR format (challenge, action, result). You'll use these stories again in an interview, but you will add one more element to your story: the context or situation. We call it the SOAR technique because it includes the *situation* or context, an *obstacle* that required extra skills to overcome, the *actions* you took to solve the problem, and the *results* that benefited the organization.

So when interviewing, build your stories around SOAR: situation, obstacle, actions, and results.

- **Verifiable, not just an opinion:** If you have a professional certificate, that's a verifiable fact. Great communication skills are less concrete, so they may not be such a good key selling point unless you can offer some form of evidence, such as related experience in your resume, a writing sample, or a sound bite from a LinkedIn recommendation.

Prepare to communicate your key selling points memorably. Think about this: What do we remember?

- **We remember what comes first and last.** Emphasize your key selling points in your first interview answer—generally, your answer to "tell me about yourself"—and in your closing remarks.
- **We remember what is reinforced.** Make some reference to your key selling points in your follow-up messages.
- **We remember what is vivid**—what we can see in our mind's eye. Illustrate your key selling points with stories.

Here's an example, told by a candidate for a sales manager job.

SOAR Story: Tripling Sales Leads

When I was sales manager at Terrific Technology, we had a third-party call center that was supposed to pass along leads to our inside sales team, but we were only getting about 10 leads a day. (The Situation)

So I decided to work closely with the call center reps. There was initially some resistance because they had their own methods. So I called their manager in Bangalore and got to know him, listened to his concerns, and collaborated with him to figure out how to make it work. We negotiated methods and schedules that worked for both of us. (Obstacle and Actions)

I then improved their scripts, provided a sales training webinar, and coached some of the reps one-on-one. (More Actions)

Within a month, the flow of leads went up to 30 a day, which increased revenue by at least $50,000 that year. (The Results)

How Does SOAR Help?

SOAR reminds you to organize your thoughts so that your stories are complete, compelling, and concise. SOAR also teaches you to make sure you include results. The most common mistake in interview storytelling is to shortchange the results. Many people telling this story would end with, "So I improved their scripts, provided a sales training via webinar, and coached some of the reps one-on-one."

"Hmm," thinks the interviewer, "So you spent a lot of time, but did it *work*?"

Be specific about results. Quantifying can really help: Say how fast, how much, or how many hours saved or dollars earned. If you don't have exact figures, estimate.

Develop Your Stories List

Start compiling a list of stories, especially stories that illustrate your key selling points. Having trouble remembering stories? Find lists of behavioral interview questions online, and they'll help jog your memory.

Try to build your list to at least a dozen stories, and preferably 20 or more. In today's lengthy interview processes, you may be asked dozens of questions. You don't want to have to tell the same handful of stories over and over.

Don't write your stories out as full scripts because that will make you sound over-rehearsed and result in a huge list that's hard to review quickly. Instead, for each story simply write down a title and a few points you might otherwise forget to mention.

Then list the skills and strengths the story demonstrates. Now, if an interviewer asks about a particular skill, you'll know which story to tell.

Use the template in Figure 14-1 to start your story list. This will be one of your most powerful job search tools.

```
Title:

Be sure to mention:

Skills and strengths this story illustrates:
```

SOAR Stories List Template.

Tell Me About Yourself

Because it comes first, "would you tell me about yourself " may be the most important question in the whole interview. Build your answer around your key selling points, and you'll have an answer that shows you're the right person for the job.

For example, Claudia Candidate is interviewing for a job as an instructional designer. Following the instructions provided earlier in this chapter, she has identified the following as her key selling points:

- 10 years of progressively responsible training department experience leading up to her most recent role as a lead instructional designer.
- Strong accomplishments.
- Exceptional motivation to work for this company: She has been talking with people from this company and watching for openings for a year; working there is her dream.
- An MA in instructional design.
- Web design and graphic design skills above and beyond the requirements.

Her answer to "tell me about yourself " could sound something like this:

I'm really excited to be here because I use all your apps and I've been following Cool Company for a long time. I was thrilled to be referred to you by Shandra Smith.

As you can see in my resume, I've been working in training departments for 10 years, and I've progressed through various positions up to my recent role as lead instructional designer at XYZ company.

I've made a real difference there. For example, last year I led an overhaul of our sales training programs for 600 reps nationwide. Participant ratings went up from 7 to 9.5 out of 10, and the reps started performing better, which led to revenue growth.

Some of my other strengths include web design and graphic design skills and a master's in instructional design from QRS University, which gives me a solid grounding in [here she names a couple of hard-to-find skills relevant to the opening].

For me, the most motivating thing about designing training programs is finding out that people are actually doing their jobs better and enjoying them more because of what I created. That's always my goal.

Working here sounds like a perfect fit with what I'm looking for. I've talked to several people connected to the company, and I like what I've heard about the culture and where you're going. Do you have any questions about what I've said so far?

Elements of a Good "Tell Me About Yourself" Answer

When crafting a good "tell me about yourself " answer, try to include most or all of these elements:

- an opening that gets the interviewer's interest
- focus on key selling points
- a very brief career summary
- an accomplishment example, demonstrating that you get results
- a little work-relevant insight into your motivations and personality
- a brief statement of your well-informed enthusiasm about the job
- a good question at the end (the one in the example is ideal—feel free to use it).

Then practice saying it. To make sure you don't sound robotic or over-rehearsed, don't memorize a script. Instead, create a simple outline or list of your key talking points (but don't write it out in full sentences). Talk through your answer, referring to your outline, until you can say it from memory. Then practice with a partner, asking him to tell you what he liked best about your answer and what could be better. Keep working on it until you feel confident that your answer will leave employers with a clear sense of why they should hire you—and an interest in hearing more!

Prepare for Common Interview Questions

Plan your answers to common interview questions (which you can easily find online), as well as others you know they'll ask based on your resume, such as "How did you win this award?" or "Why is there a gap in your work history?" Create a list of typical questions and jot down a few notes under each as needed. As with your "tell me about yourself " outline, keep your notes brief. When you're preparing for a specific interview, you can look up the company on Glassdoor.com to see if past interviewees posted interview questions there.

Use every answer to market yourself for the job by keeping the focus on your key selling points. Every answer should show employers why they should hire you.

Sometimes it's not obvious what an interview question is really about, so you should get in the habit of asking yourself, "What are they really trying to find out here?"

Notice when the question requires a story. If it starts with a phrase such as "tell me about a time when" or "give me a specific example of," then a general answer isn't enough. Even if specific stories and examples are not asked for, use them frequently. SOAR

stories will make your answers more believable *and* memorable.

Make sure you are authentic in your answers. Lies and exaggerations will probably come back to haunt you, and answers "borrowed" from websites can sound phony. Be strategic and be real.

One important question to prepare for is, "What are your salary expectations?" This is often asked in phone screenings, which can occur unexpectedly. In general, you should try to delay answering this question until later in the interview process. However, if pressed, it's best to provide a range that is based on your research of your market value. This issue is covered in detail in chapter 11, so review it for further guidance on handling salary questions. Plan and rehearse your answer carefully, because it can affect your earnings for years to come.

Once you're in the interview, listen carefully! Make sure you understand what the interviewer is asking. If you're not sure, ask a clarifying question. Don't repeat yourself. Once you've said what you need to say, stop. Table 14-1 addresses commonly asked interview questions and what the interviewer is looking for.

TABLE 14-1. Common Interview Questions and What They're Really About

The Question	What They're Looking For
"What's your story?"	• Why should we hire you? • Do you have the good judgment to handle this strange question and give me an answer that's relevant?
"Tell me about your current or past job."	• How did that job prepare you for this one?
"What's your biggest weakness?"	• Is it a weakness so serious it disqualifies you? • Are you transparent about areas in which you need to improve? • Do you strive for continuous improvement?
"Tell me about a time when you failed."	• Are you open and honest? • Do you learn from your failures? • Do you do everything you can to "save the day"?
"Tell me about your best boss ever."	• Do you value a boss who makes you stretch and grow, or one who's just easy? • Have you worked well with past managers?
"Tell me about a difficult person you had to work with."	• Are you able to work well with everyone? • Are you fair and nonjudgmental, or do you get caught up in complaining? • Can you answer this sensitive question discreetly, without damaging someone else's reputation (or your own)?
"Are you having other interviews?"	• Are you about to take another job? • Are we wasting our time interviewing you?
"Where do you see yourself in five years?"	• If we hire you, will you stay a reasonable amount of time? • Will you grow and take on more responsibility? • Are you realistic and patient about seeking advancement?
"Who are our competitors?"	• Do you understand our market position and our challenges? • Are you interested enough to try to find out?
"How would you describe the color yellow to a blind person?"	• Can you show us you're comfortable with ambiguity and unexpected challenges? • Can you demonstrate certain soft skills relevant to this job (e.g., creativity, intuition, and communication skills)?

Impress by Asking Good Questions

Acing an interview is not just about giving the right answers. Asking the right questions is crucial. Good questions show that you're seriously interested in the job, and that you're already thinking ahead about how to do it well. Failing to ask questions will make you seem uninterested.

It's important to prepare 10 or 12 questions for the end of the interview. You won't actually ask that many, but you need plenty because some may have already been answered by that point.

The end of the interview isn't the only time to ask questions. Asking questions early can arm you with information that helps you sell your skills, because the more you know about the employer's needs, goals, and activities, the better you can target your message.

Think about this. A good question:

- shows good communication skills and a sense of appropriateness
- focuses on the work, not the pay: until the company has made you an offer, never ask about compensation, benefits, flextime, or perks
- shows that you've done your homework: the best questions are grounded in the research you've done on the company. For example, "I've

read articles about your company's new push for online self-service. How is that affecting this department?"

Any of the following questions could be customized and improved by referring to what you already know:

- What are the most important aspects of this role?
- Can you describe a typical day in this role?
- What are the goals and priorities for this role?
- Is this a new position?
- If not, what happened to the person who was previously in the job?
- What changes are ahead for this company in the coming year, and in the next few years?
- What are the greatest strengths and weaknesses of this company?
- What do you love about working here? Why have you stayed at this company?
- What do you find frustrating about working here?
- How would you describe the company culture, and how is it evolving?

These questions are good to ask a recruiter:

- What is the name and title of the person I would be reporting to in this role?
- What kind of person works best with him or her?
- What's the next step after our conversation today?

These questions are appropriate to ask the hiring manager (your prospective boss):

- What are your goals for this role? If I were successful, what would that look like?
- What are the top priorities for this role in the first 60 days?
- How does upper management view the role and the impact of this department?
- What training, development, and recognition have your reports received in the past year?
- What is your management style?

You could ask these questions to members of senior management:

- How does this department contribute to the growth of the company?
- How do you see this department's role changing as the company grows?
- How is this company looking to evolve so it continues to compete effectively? • How could a person in this role support that evolution?

We've looked at how to answer questions and how to ask them, but only in terms of words. Now let's look at the important dimension beyond the verbal.

Nonverbal Communication and "Chemistry"

Employers don't make hiring decisions on a purely rational basis. A lot of it comes down to gut feelings, and nonverbal communication has a big influence. Some experts say two-thirds of communication is nonverbal. So, what do you need to do to make sure you're giving off the right vibes? Get feedback on your nonverbals.

Your first step is to look in a mirror or videotape yourself while you practice. This way you can see what you look like and gain some perspective. However you also need an outside perspective, so ask a friend or

coach to do mock interviews with you. Ask for critique about not just what you said, but the overall impression you give. How was your handshake, smile and other facial expressions, eye contact, posture, movement, tone of voice, and appearance? What did you do well and what could use improvement?

Much has been written about body language—more than will fit into this chapter—so for now, let's look at some of the most important points.

First Things First

The interviewer's first in-person impression of you is likely to involve a smile, eye contact, and a handshake.

When you are practicing, give special attention to these actions. Ask a friend for feedback.

Mind Your Posture

In most cases good posture means sitting up straight and leaning forward slightly, with both feet on the floor or with your legs crossed all the way; avoid resting your ankle on your knee, which looks too casual. Your hands

can be in your lap, or sometimes gesturing. But don't cross your arms because it can make you seem standoffish; you want to look open and receptive.

Say the Interviewer's Name

Most people like to hear their own name, so use it when shaking hands at the beginning and end of the interview, and maybe once or twice in between.

Should you say "John" or "Mr. Jones"? The etiquette on this is changing, and not everyone agrees on it. One common view is that it's best to follow the interviewer's cues: If she calls you by your first name, reply in the same way. Other experts say it's better to address the interviewer formally until they specifically invite you to use their first name. Use the approach that seems to fit your particular situation.

Dress to Impress

What to wear depends on many factors—the role, the industry, and the company. As a general rule, dress one level higher than the way you would dress on the job.

If the workplace is casual (jeans, T-shirts, athletic shoes), come to the interview in business casual: dress slacks, a skirt or a dress, an open-collared shirt, semi-dress shoes, and maybe a blazer. If business casual is the standard workplace attire, wear a suit—preferably blue or gray, closed-toe dress shoes, and if you're a man put on a tie. If you'll be wearing a suit every day, you can't get much dressier than that. Wear a suit.

Etiquette

An interview is more formal than most day-to-day situations, so watch your manners even before you walk into the building and as you reach your car afterward. Here are some things you may not have thought of:

- Wait to be offered a seat before sitting down, or at least wait until the others have taken their seats.
- If offered a beverage other than water, it may best to politely decline. This is considerate to your host. Also, nervous people are more accident-prone, and you don't want to risk spilling coffee on yourself or your host's furniture! Water is simpler and safer.
- Don't place personal items—briefcase, water bottle, and so forth—on the interview table. Instead, put them under your chair or on an empty chair next to you. You may place a portfolio or notepad and pen on the table if you bring one.
- Don't just turn off your cell phone—put it out of sight.
- As of this writing, it is still inadvisable to take notes on an electronic device at an interview.
- When leaving the interview, if possible, stop in the outer office and thank the person who greeted you when you arrived.

Interview Formats: Know How to Ace Them All

Not every job interview is a one-on-one, question-and-answer session. There are many interview formats, and each has its own challenges and opportunities. Reduce the "surprise factor" by knowing how to succeed in any format.

Phone Screening

A phone screening can be a little like a "pop quiz"—it may arrive out of the blue. So as soon as you've sent in your resume, get ready. Keep all job announcements you've applied to readily available, along with your cover letters and resumes. When a recruiter calls and says he's calling about *X* company, you don't want to be struggling to remember, "Which job was that? What did I tell them about myself?" Having these materials handy helps keep you prepared.

The recruiter may subtly pressure you to "talk for a few minutes *right now*" even though it's not a good time for you. Asking to reschedule may put you at a disadvantage, because a busy recruiter may simply move on to other candidates. However, if it really is a bad time, it may be better to ask, "Is there another time we can talk today?" rather than do a poor interview because you're distracted.

In any phone interview, your tone of voice is crucial. Make a point of smiling, which can be heard in your voice, and stand up, which makes your voice sound more energetic.

One-on-One, Face-to-Face

This type of interview is familiar to most of us. Typically longer than a phone screening, an in-person interview may be a half hour, an hour, or longer. (A lengthy interview is often a good sign!)

Did you know that being more than 15 minutes early to an in-person interview can actually make a bad impression? It's smart to get to the interview location well in advance to ensure you won't be late, but wait in a coffee shop or in your car until 10 to 15 minutes before the scheduled time. Use this extra time to review your notes about the job, the people, and what you plan to say. You can also do your relaxation exercises and visualize a successful interview.

When you go inside, pay attention for clues about the company culture and what it's like working there. Be friendly, but not too chatty, with the receptionist and whoever else you encounter.

Panel Interview

Panel interviews are usually intended to standardize the interviewing process, so they are firmly structured. Often, several interviewers are lined up across from you, taking turns asking prepared questions. The situation may feel artificial and not very comfortable, but look at it this way: The interviewers probably don't enjoy it either. Let that thought give you a feeling of empathy toward them. Try to be gracious and put them at ease, and you may end up making yourself feel more relaxed as well.

As you answer the interview questions, include all the interviewers in your gaze and body language—not just the person who asked the question. And don't only focus on the friendly people; the grumpy one needs to be convinced, too.

If note taking is allowed, write down the name and role of each person present. Arrange the names on your notepad in the same way the people are arranged in the room—Kyle on the left, Lisa on the right—this will help you remember who is who. If possible, exchange business cards.

Group Interview

The term *group interview* can mean different things, but here we'll focus on a process in which multiple candidates interact together in a round-table discussion or small-group exercise. This format allows interviewers to observe interpersonal skills such as teamwork, leadership, and helping to facilitate the stated goals of the exercise.

It's a balancing act: Demonstrate your skills without taking over, and collaborate with people who may also be your competitors as you might do on the job if you were competing with teammates for a promotion while still working together for a common goal.

Behavioral Interview

Behavioral interview questions generally start with language such as "tell me about a time when" and require you to tell a specific story from your experience. Some interviewers rely heavily on such questions. The theory behind behavioral interviewing is that your behavior and performance in the past is the best predictor of how you'll perform if hired. So, as stated earlier in this chapter, it's important to develop a list of success stories that you can draw from to answer these questions.

Sequential or All-Day Interviews

It is increasingly common to have multiple interviews for a single position, and when they're crammed into one day it can be a bit mind-boggling. It is important to fight the fatigue! You may want to bring along a bottle of tea or a snack such as a protein bar.

In each interview, vary the stories and examples you tell because interviewers may compare notes later. If possible, take a few notes after each interview, before it all begins to blur together. This will help you write smart follow-up messages later.

Meal Interview

A meal with your prospective boss and teammates may not be called an interview, but it can have the same effect on your candidacy, so prepare. Plan your order in advance to save time. Order a very light meal so you can concentrate on communicating rather than eating. Avoid alcoholic beverages, even if the boss is drinking. Keep your phone off and out of sight. Be polite to restaurant staff.

Should you socialize or get down to business? Follow the lead of your host. One good conversation strategy is to ask the others what they enjoy most about their work and the company. Relax, but don't be caught off guard and be on your best behavior as to conversational topics and table manners—even if the boss is less correct!

Testing

Various types of tests may be given at interviews, including aptitude tests, which could involve anything from basic skills of reading, writing, or math to computer or technical skills, as well as behavioral or personality tests.

It's best to be honest in personality tests because they are designed to spot dishonesty. However, it may be helpful to take practice tests in advance. The Dummies website (www.dummies.com) is a great resource for practice personality tests. Chapter 10 covers pre-employment testing in great detail, so review it for more guidance on this topic.

Case Interview

Case interviews are a specific type of testing. In a case interview, candidates are given a situation or problem similar to one they would face on the job and asked to resolve it. Many webpages and books have been written on this type of interview, and this chapter cannot begin to cover the subject.

If invited to this type of interview, plan to spend many hours preparing for it, over a period of many days if possible. You can read more about case interviews on websites such as www.LiveCareers.com and www.Vault.com.

Presentation-Facilitation Interview

You may be asked to develop and give a presentation, either on a topic of your choice or one selected by the interviewer. If your work involves training, you may be asked to facilitate a short workshop. Others within the company may join as an audience or active participants.

Of course you need to demonstrate your knowledge, but strive to make it enjoyable for others as well. Make it interesting and encourage comments and interaction. Use appropriate humor to put people at ease.

Video Interviews

Although many employers use video interviewing, few people really enjoy the process. Even the interviewers are likely to be uncomfortable. If you can make the experience feel more natural, engaging, and enjoyable for all concerned, you will stand out and make a good impression. Video interviews may be either two-way calls or asynchronous. Two-way calls happen in real time, typically through platforms such as Skype or Google Hangouts. In an asynchronous interview, you're not interacting with an interviewer in real time; instead, you are sent a list of questions and record your responses.

You should familiarize yourself with the technology. Test it out in advance if possible, and make sure you understand what to do before you start. It is also important to make sure your face is well lit. Look at yourself through your computer's Photo Booth or Crazy Cam application, through a camera, or even in a mirror,

to see how your face is lit. Then adjust the lighting in the room as necessary.

Make sure you're looking directly into the camera because this creates the effect of eye contact. If the camera isn't at eye level, adjust its position. If you're using a laptop, put a box or books under it to raise it.

To really master digital interviewing, refer to Paul Bailo's book, *The Essential Digital Interview Handbook: Lights, Camera, Interview: Tips for Skype, Google Hangout, GoToMeeting, and More.*

"Wow Factor" Extras

Whatever type of interview you're participating in, consider demonstrating that you're the kind of employee who goes above and beyond by sharing something extra, such as a portfolio, PowerPoint presentation, or a 30-60-90-day plan showing how you will create value if hired.

Your portfolio could include work samples, summaries of projects, graphs and other visual aids, letters of recommendation, copies of certificates or recognitions, transcripts, or highly favorable performance evaluations, as well as your resume and references.

If you've prepared a presentation to show on a computer, make sure it can be simply and instantly

displayed on your laptop or tablet without any need for additional equipment or setup.

If you bring a 30-60-90-day plan, make sure it is customized to the specific job and company, thoroughly researched, and brief—no more than four pages.

Know that some interviewers may not want to look at these extra items, so try to find out in advance whether they're welcome. Whatever you bring, choose the right moment to use it. A good time might be when the employer has asked a question related to the items you've brought.

Closing the Interview

You've marketed your skills impressively from the first handshake to the last question and the interviewer is wrapping it up. You're done, right? Not quite. Remember, you want to be remembered as the best person for the job—and in addition to first impressions, final impressions are memorable as well. So it is important to reiterate your key selling points and your interest in the job.

Remember Claudia, the instructional designer from earlier in this chapter? Here's what her closing statement sounded like:

Thank you again for your time today. I'm even more excited than before. Your plan for the new

training portal sounds exactly like the type of project where my web design and graphic skills can be a big asset. And overall, I've got the experience and education to lead your design team credibly and be a great resource. I think it's a great fit and I'd love to join your team!

Assuming they don't hire Claudia on the spot, she should then ask about next steps, including whether it would be okay to call on such-and-such day to follow up.

Follow Up Right—Not by Rote

Most candidates send a brief thank you note after an interview. But if you want to stand out, make sure your follow-up communications reinforce the reasons why you're the right person for the job. The purposes of the follow-up thank you note are to:

- Express appreciation.
- Reiterate your strong interest in the position.
- Remind the employer of your key selling points.
- Add a bit more information—another accomplishment, for example—or to correct a misimpression.

Should you send a handwritten note, an email, or a typed letter? Each has its advantages, and the impact depends on your industry. A handwritten note could seem old-fashioned in some industries, but could be a good way to stand out in others. Whatever form it takes, make sure your message arrives soon, preferably by the next business day.

Then stay on their radar screen. Additional written messages, or possibly a phone call, can help demonstrate that you're highly motivated and assertive. Take a helpful tone—"I wanted to see whether you need any additional information"—rather than asking whether they've made a decision.

Checklist: What to Bring to the Interview

As we approach the end of this chapter, you've probably noticed that there is a lot to remember about interviewing. Use this checklist to keep track of your logistics on the big day. Add or delete items to adapt the list to your own unique situation.

- Pen and notepad
- List of questions you want to ask
- Copies of your resume and cover letter
- Copies of up to three letters of recommendation
- Notes to review beforehand (for example, SOAR stories, talking points in response to common questions)
- Job posting, names of people you'll meet, any other details you have about the interview
- Master application to copy information from
- Carrying case (folder or briefcase)
- Address, directions (including an alternate route), and a map (paper or app)
- Cash for alternate transportation, just in case
- Plan B for wardrobe malfunction (spare tie, safety pin, spare nylons, makeup)
- Cell phone, off
- Optional: Portfolio, presentation, or 30-60-90-day plan.

Summary

Acing the interview is not simple; in any type of interview—from the shortest phone screening to an all-day interview on-site—there are many opportunities to answer the unspoken question, "Why should we hire you?"

You can demonstrate you're the one to hire by:

- initiating rapport with a firm handshake, eye contact, and a smile
- memorably communicating your key selling points right from the start
- effectively telling SOAR stories so the employer can easily visualize the skillful way you do your work
- nailing every detail, from appropriate clothing to what you brought (and didn't bring) with you
- marrying authenticity with strategy to sell your skills with every answer.

Successfully interviewing takes work. Reading this chapter was a great start, and now comes the most important part: Go through it again and act on every tip that applies to you. Plan and practice like the smart, hard-working professional you are! Because most candidates don't prepare enough, you will stand out and be remembered. Get ready for a job offer!

The Elevator Speech

The term "elevator speech" refers to a hypothetical situation in which you enter an elevator and realize you're standing next to an executive who works for a prestigious company. In such a situation, you would only have thirty seconds to a minute to introduce yourself and make an impression. To do so, you need to deliver a concise yet detailed speech that explains who you are and what makes you unique, compared to your competition.

Although you won't often find yourself in that specific situation, you will have multiple opportunities to deliver an effective elevator speech, including at networking events and at interviews when a recruiter asks, "Tell me about yourself."

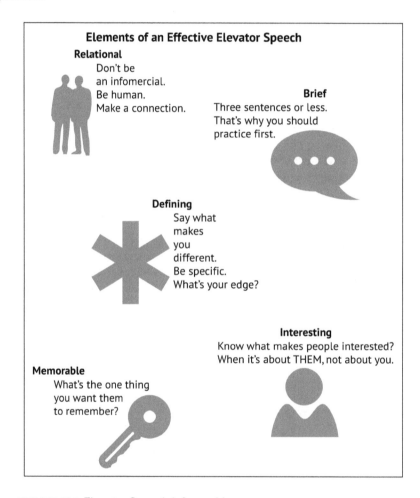

FIGURE 14.1 Elevator Speech Infographic.

Source: Freakishlyproductive.com.

Assignment: Write an Elevator Speech

To prepare for interviews and networking events, draft your own elevator speech. Every elevator speech is unique to the individual delivering it, but here are some general principles that can help you write your speech:

Drafting Your Elevator Speech

1. Introduction
   a. Establish listener's attention (friendly feeling and curiosity)
2. Body
   a. Where you've been (past)
   b. Where you are now (present)
   c. Where you're going (goals for future)
3. Conclusion
   a. Call to action (goal, next steps, referral, appointment, etc.)

For this course, you will write and rehearse an elevator speech. You will want to practice your speech until you can deliver it smoothly. Then you will deliver your elevator speech in class as well as during your mock interview.

Behavioral Interviewing Questions

Most people are nervous when they go into an interview situation and so are often unable to present themselves in the best way possible. Practice is one of the most common suggestions for succeeding in interviews, and often students who participate in many interviews testify to how much the repetition improves their performance.

You probably know that most companies use "behavioral interview questions" to help determine if a candidate will be a good fit for the position. One way to shine in your interview (and reduce your nerves) is to prepare for the most common behavioral interviewing questions and practice answering them.

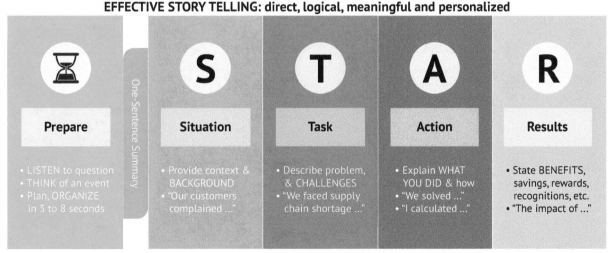

EFFECTIVE STORY TELLING: direct, logical, meaningful and personalized

Prepare	One-Sentence Summary	Situation	Task	Action	Results
• LISTEN to question • THINK of an event • Plan, ORGANIZE in 5 to 8 seconds		• Provide context & BACKGROUND • "Our customers complained ..."	• Describe problem, & CHALLENGES • "We faced supply chain shortage ..."	• Explain WHAT YOU DID & how • "We solved ..." • "I calculated ..."	• State BENEFITS, savings, rewards, recognitions, etc. • "The impact of ..."

Do not think of new details as you answer. SAY what you had planned for & END

FIGURE 14.2 STAR Infographic.

Source: (Hourglass) Copyright © 2012 Depositphotos/MyVector.

Interviewers are looking for specific elements in your responses to behavioral interviewing questions. The article you read uses the acronym SOAR (Situation, Obstacle, Actions, Results) to define these steps; another common acronym is STAR (Situation, Task, Action, Result).

Interviewers who use behavioral interviewing questions typically ask questions about:

- Leadership
- Communication
- Teamwork or working with difficult people
- Conflict or solving problems
- Failure
- Overcoming adversity
- Stress/time management
- Greatest accomplishment
- Weakness

To prepare for a variety of questions using a variety of situations, complete the exercise below ("Activity: Log of Accomplishments and Stories"). Then you will have an opportunity to practice answering behavioral interview questions using the SOAR/STAR method.

Applying This Skill: Log of Accomplishments & Stories

Successful resumes, cover letters, and interviews will include details about specific situations. To prepare for the job search, develop a list of accomplishments and situations you might use to respond to interview questions. Mine the following settings for stories: work, education, volunteering, extracurricular activities, group memberships, etc. For each of the topics listed below, write 1–2 ideas/specific situations. This will help you develop situations to use with the STAR interviewing method.

1. Ways you have worked effectively in a team

_____

_____

_____

_____

2. Problems or challenges you've overcome and how you overcame them

_____

_____

_____

_____

3. Accomplishments you are most proud of and why

_____

_____

_____

_____

4. Ways you've demonstrated leadership

_____

_____

_____

_____

5. What motivates you?

_____

_____

_____

_____

6. Failures and/or weaknesses and how you managed them

_____

_____

_____

_____

7. Communication and/or conflict resolution skills

_____

_____

_____

_____

8. Your greatest strengths

_____

_____

_____

_____

9. Honors, accomplishments, praise

_____

_____

_____

_____

10. Any other stories/situations that may be useful in answering interview questions

_____

_____

_____

_____

Applying This Skill: Peer Interview Practice

In this activity, you will pair with one or most of your peers to practice asking and answering behavioral interviewing questions. During one round, you will be the interviewee and practice answering questions based on the SOAR/STAR method and using the situations and stories you developed in the "Activity: Log of Accomplishments and Stories."

During another round, you will be the interviewer. When you are the interviewer, please ask the following questions:

1. Tell me a little about yourself (this is where the interviewee should use his/her elevator speech).
2. What is your greatest weakness?
3. What is your greatest strength?
4. What motivates you?
5. How do you define success?

Then ask about as many of the following as time allows. Ask follow-up questions as appropriate.

Tell me about a time when you demonstrated or dealt with:

- Leadership
- Communication
- Teamwork
- Working with difficult people
- Conflict or solving problems
- Failure
- Overcoming adversity
- Stress/time management
- Your greatest accomplishment
- Criticism

You may also ask some of the following common interview questions:

- Why should we hire you?
- Why are you a good fit for this company?
- What are your career goals? Where do you see yourself in ten years?
- Why did you leave your last employer?
- What do you know about the company?
- Do you have any questions for me?

Assignment: Mock Interview

As part of the job application preparation process, you will complete a mock (or a real) interview during the semester. This gives you practice with your elevator speech and behavioral interviewing questions practiced in class. In addition, it helps you make connections with recruiters. Every semester, students receive internship offers that start with the mock interview process.

You will schedule an interview through your school's career services center or find someone to interview you. If you are currently interviewing for jobs or internships, you may use that interview for this assignment.

To complete the mock interview assignment, you will write a memo (following business memo format) summarizing your preparation, the interview itself (including questions asked and how you answered), the lessons learned you learned, and the value of the experience to you. Specifics about content to include in the memo appear below.

PREPARATION AND NOTES

Before the interview, write at least one paragraph for each of the following:

- **Know yourself:** What are your interests, abilities, personality, and values? How do these fit the position that interests you? Be able to explain why you are interested in your career field of interest.
- **Research the organization.** Review the employer's website. Pay attention to their "about us" section. Look for their mission statement and news about the company. Who are they? What are their major products or services? Be able to discuss any of this with the interviewer.
- **Research a position on that company's website** and/or a position that you would be suited for as an internship opportunity and/or a first career position. Be able to name one position for which they hire new college graduates. Identify a few of the key qualifications for their position (or for the position you would like to obtain). Match your qualifications to the job position so you can speak to how you will add value to the company.
- **Prepare questions**, based on your research, that you will ask the interviewer.

ATTEND THE MOCK INTERVIEW

- Arrive a few minutes early.
- Dress professionally.
- Bring one to two copies of your resume.
- Act professionally; "no-shows" and late cancellations are unacceptable: they leave the employer with a negative impression of you, the business school, and the university. They also deny another student the opportunity of meeting with that employer.

REFLECTING AND WRITING

Once you have completed your mock interview, write a memo describing your experience (up to two pages long); use appropriate *memo formatting* (see Chapter 5).

In your memo, include the following:

- Information about your *preparation*, including self-reflection, company research, and questions you prepared to ask during the interview.
- Name of the *company* and the individual (name and position, time with company, etc.) who conducted the interview. Indicate the date you completed the interview.

- *Summarize* the events that happened in the mock interview. In other words, what happened in the mock interview?
    - Describe at least two questions you were asked and how you answered.
    - Name a question you asked about the company and describe the answer.
- *Describe* the feedback you received (be specific). What did the interviewer think you did well? What could you improve? If you did not receive specific feedback, analyze your own performance based on the information learned in class. What do you think you did well? What would you improve for your next interview?
- *Analyze* how the interview went and *evaluate the value* of the information and the process of conducting a mock interview for you personally. Did the interview go well? Was it a useful experience for you?

Summing Up Unit III: Preparing to Apply for a Job

Looking for a job can be a terrifying and daunting task. However, after completing Unit III, you should be well prepared, which will give you an advantage over many other job applicants. After completing Unit III, you should be able to:

- Share information, connect with people, request and write recommendations on LinkedIn
- Create a professional reference sheet
- Create a professional resume
- Write a job application cover letter
- Prepare and give an elevator speech
- Answer behavioral interviewing questions using the SOAR/STAR method

While completing this unit should give you job application documents you can use to find a job or internship right now, remember you need to update your documents for each application and continue to practice and prepare for interviews. Good luck with your job search!

Team Work and Presentations

▶ Working in Teams

▶ Oral Presentations

▶ Social Media Audit

While most people prefer to work alone, most companies and organizations use group or team work, at least part of the time. Working in groups and teams allows for successful completion of large projects because people bring different skills and talents to the group and the project may be divided into manageable pieces. Often, working together creates a synergistic energy that a single person just doesn't have; ideas may flow, skills are shared and developed, facts are checked, errors are minimized, productivity is increased and deadlines are met. Knowing how to work successfully in teams and groups is a skill that will help you throughout your career. After completing Unit IV: Working in Groups and Teams, you will have a better understanding of how to work in a group or team and have experience doing so by completing two team projects.

Either in a team or alone, the majority of business people have to give presentations at some point in their careers and some people do so frequently. Creating and delivering a presentation takes time and effort. After completing your first team project, you will understand how to create, prepare and deliver an effective presentation. The second team project focuses on social media, because many new graduates are asked to create content for or run companies' social media pages. Both team projects will help prepare you for tasks you may be asked to complete when you enter the workforce.

15   Working in Teams

Employers are always looking for people who work well in teams and work effectively as leaders. Some people are easy to work with, while others may be more challenging. Some people are natural leaders and assume that role easily, while others prefer to watch and play more supporting roles. All roles are important, and part of this course is to allow you to practice different roles in the team. After completing this lesson, you will:

- Know your team members
- Understand your leadership role and how to work in your team

Working in Teams

The ability to work effectively in a team is one of the most highly sought after skills in the business world. According to a survey done by the Society for Human Resource Management, 83% of HR professionals rated teamwork as very or extremely important when considering an applicant. Companies know that every great product, event or project is created using a team-oriented approach. Successful companies know that projects and problems are usually too large and complex for one person to manage effectively, so gathering people with a variety of skills and talents helps create positive outcomes.

What exactly is a team? A team is a small group of people working together toward a common goal. Typically, a team is comprised of members who bring unique skill sets to the group. As a result, the team is stronger as a unit. The benefits of teamwork include:

- Greater productivity
- Increased efficiency
- Increased creativity, innovation, and cooperation
- Increased performance and success
- Greater job satisfaction
- Continued personal growth and professional development

While these benefits are many, groups may also struggle with a variety of issues including struggles for leadership, the ability to give and take feedback, and effective communication.

In ineffective working groups, members may have differing goals, schedules, and work habits. Focusing on a developing a variety of communication skills will help improve members' ability to contribute to team success. To be effective team members, people need to:

- Listen carefully to others
- Contribute and explain their ideas and opinions
- Ask questions
- Participate in group discussions and communications (email/text etc.)
- Support and respect other group members

- Know tasks and meet deadlines
- Participate in group decision-making

The team projects in the course are designed to help students develop a variety of the skills needed to be effective team-members. Groups will have time to develop and share ideas, make group decisions, develop tasks, and assign deadlines. The group projects involve individual and group contributions, focus on the process of project development and revision, and sharing of leadership roles. After completing the projects in this course, students should have developed some of the teamwork skills so highly desired by HR professionals.

Source: SHRM/Mercer Survey Findings: Entry-Level Applicant Job Skills, SHRM 2016
https://www.shrm.org/hr-today/trends-and-forecasting/research-and-surveys/

Applying This Skill: Get to Know Your Team

After your new team members exchange names, make a list of four to five silly, crazy, and unusual questions. The more unusual, the better. You may not ask the typical questions involving year in school, major, jobs, etc. You don't need to answer the questions; just think of them and write them down.

Assignment: Team Leadership Roles

In this course, each student will lead a major team assignment. Your job as leader will be to establish timelines, tasks, roles/responsibilities, quality standards, etc. In addition, you will be responsible for compiling each person's portion of the project, proofreading it, and submitting the team's assignment. Each person will be the team leader at a different time during the semester. This allows people who tend to avoid leadership roles to practice that position and forces people who typically take charge to relinquish the role to others. Both are important skills to have in the workforce.

In this course, your team will complete two projects: an oral research presentation and a social media audit. The leadership roles are named according to the task the team member will coordinate. The Bibliography and Presentation Visuals leaders will coordinate aspects of the team's research project. The Progress Report, Letter, and Posts leaders will coordinate aspects of the team's social media project (these roles are *not* related to the research project).

After reading the descriptions, decide who in your team will fulfill each of the following leadership roles. Write down who will be responsible for each role and submit that to your instructor. The leadership roles are:

- Bibliography: Annotated Bibliography
  Expertise: Secondary research
  Responsible for: Compiling annotated bibliography

- Presentation Visuals: PPT/Prezi
  Expertise: Presentation visuals, graphics
  Responsible for: Compiling presentation visuals

- Progress Report: Progress Report
  Expertise: Report writing
  Responsible for: Compiling/writing progress report

- Letter: Letter to Client
  Expertise: Writing
  Responsible for: Compiling/writing letter to client

- Posts: Social Media Posts
  Expertise: Social media
  Responsible for: Compiling/writing sample posts for client

16   Giving Oral Presentations

Team Project One: Team Oral Presentation

While most college students take a speech course at some point in their educational careers, many do not have instruction on giving business presentations, but over half of business graduates are presenting on a monthly to weekly basis. This course is designed to help you develop, plan, and deliver a presentation effectively. After completing this lesson, you will:

- Know how to plan an oral presentation using brainstorming and organizational planning
- Know how to prepare an oral presentation using audience analysis and purpose
- Learn and demonstrate best practices for use of visuals in presentations
- Create and edit visual presentations
- Practice research skills
- Identify and use credible business trade journals
- Summarize articles and present information concisely

Your instructor will assign you to a team. Your team will be required to research and give an oral presentation on a topic as assigned by your instructor. Presentations should have an overall theme, introduction, and conclusion and should be developed considering your audience.

Each person will speak for 4–5 minutes. Dress is business professional or nice business casual.

Your team will prepare a visual presentation to accompany your oral presentation.

Completing the readings and exercises in this chapter and following the "Steps to an Effective Presentation" will help you prepare and present an effective team oral presentation.

Reading 16.1

Why Must I Give a Memorable Presentation?

Getting Started the Right Way

By Jason L. Snyder and Robert Forbus

Before you begin preparing your presentation ask yourself this simple question, what is my presentation about? If you answer that question with one or two words, then you skipped Chapter 3, where we talked about purpose statements. We won't force you to go back and read it now, but we do want you to understand one important point. World-class consultant and author Nancy Duarte reminds her followers that presentations are your opportunity to change your part of the world, even in business. Before you start putting together your presentation, you need to identify your "big idea": What idea are you selling to your audience and what are the stakes involved? You need to get out of the routine of saying, "my presentation is about increasing sales." Instead, get into the habit of expressing your big idea with the stakes involved. Try the following: "We need to adopt new sales strategies or we will be driven out of business."[1] Instead of thinking about topics you will discuss, think about how your big ideas will change your world.

Figure 16.1 summarizes a number of techniques you might use to energize the introduction to a presentation.

1. Ask a question	6. Make a startling statement
2. Tell a story	7. Tell a personal anecdote
3. Find a quotation	8. Use humor
4. Use a visual aid	9. Reference expert opinion
5. Cite a statistic	10. Tell a success story

FIGURE 16.1 Ten techniques for making a powerful introduction.

Supercharging Your Introduction

How many times have you witnessed someone who gets up before a group, gives his or her name, states the topic, and launches immediately into the material? Dozens? Hundreds? Thousands? For us, it's been in the high hundreds, for sure. By this point in our lives, the lazy introduction is the quickest way to make us grab our iPads and start updating our Facebook pages or checking our various email accounts. We simply believe if you do not care enough to make a compelling introduction that captures our attention, we do not care enough to leave our iPads alone. The tips that follow, and in Figure 16.1, will help you supercharge your introduction and capture your audience's attention.

Don't limit yourself to using only one of the tips. Many introductions will use more than one of these tips:

Ask a Question

We like this approach least, because it's easy, but it is certainly better than no introduction at all. If you take this approach, make your question rhetorical or provocative. Anticipate the response you will get from the audience. We have seen too many presentations fall apart because the speaker asked a question and the audience didn't provide a response.

Tell a Story

We find stories about something you've read or something you've seen or someone you've known to be highly effective. Just make sure the story relates clearly to your topic. Stories not only engage your audience, but you can leave them with a cliffhanger you will return to in the presentation's conclusion.

Find a Quotation

We regularly thumb through online books of quotations when looking for ways to make compelling points. We figure if someone else has said it, and it's good enough to be in a book of quotations, then it's good enough for us. Plus, quotations make you look smart. Be sure to make the connection between your quote and the presentation's topic for your audience. You can even share a quotation and ask your audience questions about it if that works for you. We once delivered a presentation for a client about strategic planning. In an earlier chapter, we shared the following quote that is attributed to Dwight Eisenhower. We believe it is worth repeating: "Plans are nothing; planning is everything." We asked our audience to tell us what that meant in relation to their organization's strategic planning.

Use a Visual Aid

One of us once saw a politician begin a speech by holding up a gigantic screw made of Styrofoam and painted gold. It won't tax your imagination too much to learn that the politician was making a speech about government waste and the need to reduce taxes.

Cite a Statistic

We like Mark Twain's famous statement, "There are three types of lies—lies, damned lies, and statistics." Whether you agree with the author or not, a statistic can make a powerful point. Using statistics can be difficult because the data must really have a "wow factor." It must be truly jaw-dropping. The statistics also need to be relevant and accessible. In other words, people don't easily grasp large numbers. What do "a million smokers" look like? How large is a stack of "a trillion dollars?" It isn't really startling or dramatic if the statistic is not relevant and accessible.

Make a Startling Statement

We like these statements because they can be disruptive, provocative, or invoke laughter. There's hardly a better way to get someone's attention. Sarah Kay, the founder of Project V.O.I.C.E., delivered a now famous TED Talk. The presentation was about her work with Project V.O.I.C.E. teaching kids about the power of self-expression through spoken word poetry.[2] She said, "If I should have a daughter, instead of mom, she's gonna call me Point B, because that way she knows that no matter what happens, she can always find her way to me." These were the first words out of her mouth, and they had a profound impact on her audience. Watch her TED Talk here: http://www.ted.com/playlists/77/new_to_ted.html.

Tell a Personal Anecdote or Relay an Experience

We like these because stories are how people learn. It's the reason we've included so many in our book.

Use Humor

We like a good joke. But, we caution you to be very careful with humor. What one person laughs at, another finds incredibly offensive. Save your best retelling of Chris Rock jokes for your bar buddies.

Reference Expert Opinion

We like using expert opinions because it is a way to build credibility.

Tell a Success Story

We Americans love success, almost as much as we like to see successful people fail and come back from their failures. And remember, you can always use hypothetical stories, as long as that is clear with your audience.

Maximizing Your Impact

Having a supercharged introduction should get your audience engaged in your presentation. However, as we can tell you from years of experience in the classroom, getting an audience's attention and keeping it are two different things. As speakers, we need to work to keep our audience plugged in during the heart of the presentation as well. Figure 16.2 summarizes 11 ideas for keeping your audience engaged and maximizing your impact during a presentation.

1. Remember that you are the presentation	7. Do not memorize
2. Look your best	8. Demonstrate your magnetism
3. Put a smile on your face	9. Create potential
4. Demonstrate your passion	10. Empower your audience
5. Explain your purpose, then repeat and repeat again	11. Believe in yourself
6. Show your resilience	

FIGURE 16.2 Tips for maximizing your impact.

Consider how you can apply the 11 tips to improve your presentation impact:

- ***Remember that YOU are the presentation.*** Slides, handouts, leave-behinds, and other visual aids are awesome, but they aren't the presentation, YOU are.
- ***Look your best—your very best.*** People say don't judge a book by its cover, but we all do it to some degree. In fact, some research suggests that "humans can categorize others in less than 150 milliseconds."[3]
- ***Put a smile on your face.*** People who smile when they speak automatically "sound" more cheerful, warm, and approachable. Emotions, after all, are contagious.[4]
- ***Demonstrate your passion.*** If you don't show a metaphorical fire for your topic, your audience surely won't be inspired to listen and later recall your message.
- ***Explain your purpose, then repeat and repeat again.*** From the get-go, tell your audience what you want them to remember from your presentation. In your main points, reinforce what you want them to remember from your presentation. Then, when concluding, remind them again what you want them to remember.
- ***Show your resilience.*** Don't let interruptions such as questions from the audience rattle your nerves. Know your material well enough to answer questions. During a group presentation, be able to answer generally a question that might best be handled by someone else, and then hand off that question to the appropriate teammate for a more detailed response. Then, be prepared to pick back up where you left off.
- ***Do NOT memorize.*** Memorization prevents you from accomplishing number 6 above. Further, if you falter, it is very difficult to recover if you have memorized a presentation. Finally, if you memorize, you are less likely to sound conversational.
- ***Demonstrate your magnetism.*** The ability to attract money, people, and ideas is powerful, and it also helps your credibility.
- ***Create potential.*** Show your audience what is possible. They need to see the world you envision. Demonstrate the now versus the future.
- ***Empower your audience.*** Show your audience how their actions can have profoundly positive consequences. Give them the tools and guidance they need to carry out your ideas.
- ***Believe in yourself.*** Perfect practice makes perfect performance. Any athlete who is any good at his or her sport is an athlete who has done the same things over and over again, perhaps thousands of times. When you put that level of effort into your presentation, just like the athlete, you can't help but be confident.

Closing Well

You've heard them before: highly paid, very influential people ending a presentation or speech with "thank you" or "are there any questions" or, if he or she is a politician, "God bless America." Well, just because people use these closers doesn't mean these are good closing statements. It's just like when you were a child and you wanted to do something that your mother or father wouldn't allow. You might have whined, "But everyone else is doing it." And your parent(s) may have responded, "If everyone else were eating worms would you want them for dinner?" We hope you answered no. So if all these important people end their presentations with weak closing statements like the ones mentioned before, why do they do it? There are at least two reasons. First, it's not offensive. Second, it's easy.

By now, however, you've probably come to realize that we aren't big proponents of easy. This entire chapter attempts to persuade you to make a *memorable* presentation—one that the audience will recall and be influenced by well after you leave the stage, dais, or lectern. In our classes, we have adopted harsh penalties for student presentations that end in the expected way of "thank you" or "are there any questions." We encourage our students, and we encourage you, to push the limits of your comfort zone to develop memorable closing statements that summarize your major points (telling the audience what you've already told them) and reference the beginning of your presentation (tying the bow on top of the gift-wrapped box). The tips in Figure 16.3 are just a few of the many ways you can deliver a memorable closing.

---

1. If you told a story at the beginning of the presentation, return to that story and tie it to the major point(s) you want your audience to remember.
2. Find a short verse that refers to the beginning of your presentation and that gains the audience's attention through humor, empathy, sympathy, or inspiration.
3. Find a short quote from a famous person that reinforces the major points of your presentation.
4. Give a signal that you are closing. For example, "To recap the major points of my presentation, I ask you to remember ..." or "In conclusion, please remember ..."
5. Deliver a call to action. For example, "I challenge you to ..." or "Join me in ..." makes it easy for people to comply with your requests and ask them to respond quickly. The greater the distance between your request and the audience's action, the more likely they are to do nothing.

FIGURE 16.3 Tips for delivering a memorable closing.

Achieving Conversational Delivery Style

Search your memories for the most boring lecture, sermon, speech, or presentation you ever heard. We're willing to bet that one of the reasons you found it boring was the speaker didn't present in a conversational style. Public speaking blogger Olivia Mitchell and researchers Mayer, Fennell, Farmer, and Campbell (2004) agree that a conversational style, rather than a formal style, helps people learn better.[5] The late Steve Jobs, co-founder of Apple Computers, was very nearly a genius at presenting in a conversational

style. We've considered the effectiveness of three additional individuals who are typically believed to have been great 20th and 21st century communicators and have gleaned tips from their style to share with you. Our tips are based on the speaking success of Jobs, the Rev. Billy Graham, President Barack Obama, and the late President Ronald Reagan. The lessons have been packaged into the six simple ideas in Figure 16.4 that anyone can use.

1. When writing your script, imagine you are writing to one person and one person only. When proofreading your script, put the words "Hey, Joe" or "Hey, Jane" before a sentence and read it aloud to yourself. Does it sound like you're speaking to a friend?
2. When rehearsing your delivery, imagine you are speaking directly to one person and one person only. Even if your audience has thousands of people in it, you still must reach one person at a time.
3. When presenting, avoid looking at your screen if you are using one for projecting images. Rather, look at one person at a time in your audience and speak directly to him or her. If you wish, glance at your screen or gesture to it, but never speak to it.
4. When writing, and later when presenting, seek ways to connect emotionally with your audience.
5. When rehearsing, imagine the one person in your audience who will be the most difficult to reach. Spend extra time figuring out how best to reach that one hard-to-reach person (in marketing terms, this person is your target).
6. When speaking, get out from behind the lectern. How many dinner conversations have you had from behind a lectern?

FIGURE 16.4 Tips for achieving conversational delivery style.

Designing Slides and Decks for Memorable Presentations

Please don't tell Bill Gates, but we really hate Microsoft's PowerPoint software. It isn't that the product is bad. It's that the product is awful. PowerPoint has allowed people with little or no graphic design taste to create slide presentations. These presentations are sometimes referred to as "decks." Many professors and other professionals rely entirely too much on slides. How so? They simply read what is on their slides (or decks). For these situations we borrow the term "death by PowerPoint," because it describes how these excruciatingly mundane presentations bore people to death. In this section, we will give you a few pieces of simple advice that will eliminate most of the errors that create "death by PowerPoint." For a detailed treatment of slide and deck design, we recommend the work of Garr Reynolds, who wrote *Presentation Zen*, which outlines an approach where less, much less, is more.[6] If you are a nondesigner like us, then you will also find Robin Williams' book, *The Non-Designer's Design Book*, to be useful.[7]

Consider the slide in Figure 16.5. It breaks the one rule you should always follow in slide design: You are the presentation! The slides should reinforce your message, not hijack it. If your audience can read your slides, then they have no use for you.

How did the presenter end up with such a wordy slide? The main culprit is sloth. PowerPoint and similar programs are designed with default settings. When you open up a blank presentation and begin working with a slide, the bullet points are right there for you to use. How convenient. Are we wrong, or are we not sentient beings? Just because a program is set up with defaults, we are not compelled to use the defaults. Instead, we encourage you to figure out the point of each slide and to draw by hand—don't worry, we use stick figures—what you want the slide to look like. Alternatively, you can think about images that might evoke an emotional connection to the topic at hand. Once you're satisfied, open PowerPoint and try to force the program to recreate the drawing for you, or insert the image for you.

In Figure 16.6, we revised the slide from Figure 16.5. Less is more. The slide in Figure 16.6 would make an emotional connection with any audience. The audience

---

Who's Protecting the Children?

- Senator Charles Schumer of New York proposed banning the suspect baby bottles outright.
- Wal-Mart, Toys "R" Us, and CVS all announced plans to phase out polycarbonate bottles. Some companies have adopted BPA-free plastic.
- Yet most businesses stuck with BPA products—at least partly because they don't have a good substitute. Nearly all of the 130 billion food and beverage cans made in the United States each year are still lined with a BPA resin. The alternative called Oleoresin, is more expensive, has a shorter shelf life, and can't be used for acidic foods like tomatoes.
- Senator Frank Lautenberg of New Jersey has proposed an overhaul of the whole system. In May 2008, he introduced the Kid-Safe Chemical Act. The Act would reverse the burden of proof on chemicals, requiring manufacturers to demonstrate their safety in order to keep them in commerce. The E.U. passed a similar law in 2006, as did Canada in 1999. (Canada has banned BPA in baby bottles.)
- The National Toxicology Program advised "concerned parents" to reduce their use of canned foods; use BPA-free baby bottles; and opt for glass, porcelain, or stainless-steel containers, particularly for hot foods and liquids.

FIGURE 16.5 Wordy slide.

---

would much rather look at a picture of an adorable baby and listen to you provide the details. What they would dislike is listening to you read the content from the slide in Figure 16.5.

Audiences don't just dislike wordy slides; they also dislike slides with tables and graphs that have too much information. The audience cannot reasonably process complex tables and graphs and listen to you. Again, if you remember that you are the message, you will limit your tables and graphs to images that can be processed quickly so your audience will focus on what you are saying. This approach to slide design requires you to be more thoughtful about your presentation materials, but with thoughtfulness and hard work, you won't victimize your audience.

FIGURE 16.6 Revised wordy slide.

Putting It All Together

We realized people would find it helpful if we could create a set of tips that help bring together the utmost important points regarding making memorable presentations. Consequently, we developed the tips below. Initially, we used these tips for a professional development activity we conducted three consecutive years for the *Travelers EDGE* program. We liked the tips so much that we now share them with all our students. Funny enough, we can always tell which students follow these tips, and which do not. Even more funny, the students are always astounded that we can tell the difference. Those wacky students.

Notes

1. Duarte (2012).
2. Project V.O.I.C.E. (2013).
3. Elsbach (2003).
4. Hatfield, Cacioppo, and Rapson (1993).
5. Mayer, Fennell, Farmer, and Campbell (2004).
6. Reynolds (2012).
7. Williams (2004).

References

Duarte, N. (2012). *Persuasive presentations: Inspire action, engage the audience, sell your ideas.* Cambridge, MA: Harvard Business Review Press.

Elsbach, K. D. (2003). How to pitch a brilliant idea. In *HBR's 10 must reads on communication.* Cambridge, MA: Harvard Business Review Press.

Hatfield, E., Cacioppo, J. T., & Rapson, R. L. (1993). Emotional contagion. *Current Directions in Psychological Science 2,* 96–99.

Mayer, R. E., Fennell, S., Farmer, L., & Campbell, J. (2004). A personalization effect in multimedia learning: Students learn better when words are in conversational style rather than formal style. *Journal of Educational Psychology 96,* 389–395.

Project V.O.I.C.E. (2013). Retrieved June 20, 2013, from http://www.project-voice.net/

Reynolds, G. (2012). *Presentation Zen: Simple ideas on presentation design and delivery.* Berkeley, CA: New Riders.

Williams, R. (2004). *The non-designer's presentation book.* Berkeley, CA: Peachpit Press.

Develop an Oral Presentation: Team Presentation

Brainstorming

Brainstorming is a way to create and gather ideas for your team presentation. The idea is to come up with as many ideas, facts, and questions as possible. Later, you can narrow your ideas, focus them, and determine your purpose for the presentation. But now, be creative.

Nancy Duarte (2008), of Duarte Design, says your goal in a presentation is to create ideas (not slides) and move people. The first step is coming up with as many ideas as possible. Use a pencil and paper; computer programs were not designed to encourage creativity. List words, concepts, and ideas. Explore associations. Push ideas farther. Build off other people's ideas. Look at a topic from all sides. What can you discover? Go beyond the ordinary and expected. You may discover ideas or aspects of your topic that will inspire you and your audience.

You will be in a team based on a topic assigned by your instructor. In your team, write down anything you talk or think about. Be creative; go off topic, build on one another's ideas, laugh, have fun. Write each idea on a Post-it note—one idea per note. After 10–15 minutes, your team should have a poster piece of paper covered with a wide range of topics related to your team presentation.

The rules of brainstorming appear below.

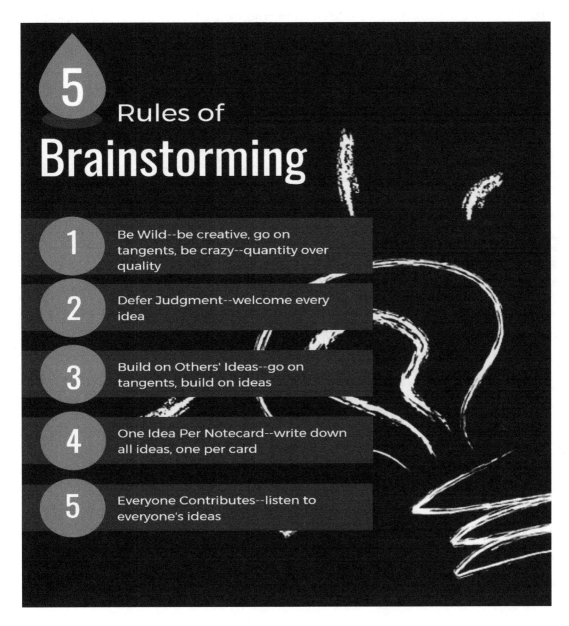

FIGURE 16.7 Brainstorming.

Plan an Oral Presentation: Audience Analysis

Any effective business communication begins with considering the audience. What does the reader need or want to know? What does the audience care about? How can you connect with them?

Nancy Duarte defines the questions you should ask about your audience while preparing an oral presentation.

Seven Questions to Knowing Your Audience

Insert a representative picture or illustration of an audience member in this rectangle. It helps to put a face on the audience.

1 What are they like?

Demographics and psychographics are a great start, but connecting with your audience means understanding them on a personal level. Take a walk in their shoes and describe what their life looks like each day.

2 Why are they here?

What do they think they're going to get out of this presentation? Why did they come to hear you? Are they willing participants or mandatory attendees? This is also a bit of a situation analysis.

3 What keeps them up at night?

Everyone has a fear, a pain point, a thorn in the side. Let your audience know you empathize—and offer a solution.

4 How can you solve their problem?

What's in it for the audience? How are you going to make their lives better?

5 What do you want them to do?

Answer the question "so what?"—and make sure there's clear action for your audience to take.

6 How can you best reach them?

People vary in how they receive information. This can include the set up of the room to the availability of materials after the presentation. Give the audience what they want, how they want it.

7 How might they resist?

What will keep them from adopting your message and carrying out your call to action?

© duarte.com 2008

FIGURE 16.8 Duarte Audience Needs Map.

Source: Duarte.com.

Applying This Skill: Audience Analysis Exercise: "The Wreck"

To explore the idea of audience, in teams complete the activity below.

The Scenario: You are a sales representative for a midsized company. You've borrowed your boss's new car to take a potential client to dinner at a fancy restaurant. If the evening goes as you plan, you'll likely finalize a large contract that is important to your company.

You are anxious and excited about the dinner reservation, but you are late. On the way, you decide to take a residential street with little traffic. The borrowed car does not have great brakes, and you want to make up some time in an area with fewer cars. Light rain and darkness are falling. In a 35 mph zone, you're going almost 50 mph.

Approaching a stop sign, you don't stop quickly enough to halt at the sign. In fact, you travel about ten feet into the intersection. You think about putting the car into reverse and backing out of the intersection, but after a quick look to the left, you think you can proceed. Just then, on your right, a car approaches rapidly and hits the borrowed car on the passenger side, ruining the door and denting the car.

Now you're really late!

Your Task: As a team, prepare a short recounting of the incident for the audience assigned. You will retell the details to your assigned audience using any form you wish (phone call, in-person conversation, letter, memo, accident report, email, text, etc.). You may choose to emphasize some details while deemphasizing others. You may make logical inferences and add some detail, but do not substantially change the facts. Draft your message (written or script, if oral) and be prepared to share it with the class. Your instructor will assign one of the audiences below.

    a. The client you were to meet for dinner, who has been in three accidents during the last year
    b. A team leader for a cross-functional company project you're working on who thinks highly of you and trusts your opinion
    c. A work associate who thinks you're always falling short and causing trouble (who is also a little jealous of your success but is liked and listened to by your boss)
    d. Your boss, owner of the wrecked car
    e. An insurance agent
    f. A lawyer who will represent you and needs to know all the "facts"
    g. A family member, friend, or spouse

Adapted from Karl Smart, "The Wreck: Meeting the Needs of the Audience,"
Business Communication Quarterly, Sept. 2000.

Applying This Skill: Audience Analysis

Audience analysis may seem simple for your college class; most of your audience members are students like you. While that's true, you should still consider the following questions. Focus on what your audience knows about the topic and how they feel about it. If you're presenting information they know about, how can you make it more relevant or new? If you're presenting information they probably don't care about, how can you make it interesting to them?

- Who are the listeners?

  _____
  _____

- What is the audience size?

  _____
  _____

- What is the average age of the audience?

  _____
  _____

- What is the male–female ratio?

  _____
  _____

- How does the audience feel about this topic? (attitude)

  _____
  _____

- How much does the audience know about the topic? What do they know?

  _____
  _____

- What expectations does the audience have about your presentation/topic?

  _____
  _____

- How will you engage the audience?

  _____
  _____

Develop an Oral Presentation: Determining a Purpose

Every presentation should have a purpose, and the purpose should be more than "This is an assignment" or "to get a good grade." Those reasons will not be relevant when you have to give presentations in the workplace. In a professional setting, a presentation's purpose may be to sell an idea or product or convince people to agree with your plan or vision.

In this class, think of your presentation as a training session. You are the experts on a certain topic and need to deliver information to the rest of the class. What do they need to know about your topic? What do you want them to remember? Why is this important to them? Developing a clear purpose will help you plan and develop an effective presentation and will ensure your audience remembers you.

Applying This Skill: Determining a Purpose

1. What is the topic of your presentation? What are your main subtopics?

_____

_____

_____

_____

_____

_____

2. What is the goal of your presentation?

_____

_____

_____

_____

_____

_____

3. What are your three main points? How do they relate to the goal?

_____

_____

_____

_____

_____

_____

4. Why does your audience care about these main points/your goal?

_____

_____

_____

_____

_____

_____

Plan an Oral Presentation: Organization

Like any communication, presentations need a clear beginning, middle, and end and transitions between topics and presenters. Starting and ending your presentation well is essential to your success. If you start by saying "Our presentation is about planning for retirement," your audience is not likely to be very excited or engaged. But if you start by saying "What does this number mean?" and showing a slide with the number $1,060,751, you're more likely to get your audience's attention. In the conclusion, revisit that startling number to summarize all of your main points. Creating clear organization, effective introductions, transitions, and conclusions takes planning but will ensure an effective and memorable presentation.

Applying This Skill: Organization

1. Draft an outline of your presentation:

2. What is your attention-getting introduction?

3. What is your conclusion?

4. Where will you be presenting? What is the facility like? What are the visual aid/technology options?

5. How much time is allotted for your presentation?

_____

_____

_____

_____

_____

_____

_____

_____

_____

6. Who speaks before/after you? How will you transition between speakers?

_____

_____

_____

_____

_____

_____

_____

_____

_____

Plan an Oral Presentation: Do Your Research

When giving a business presentation, you need to provide your audience with credible, valuable information, so you need to do your research. In the future, you may need to read trade journals aimed at industry insiders, company reports, legal briefs or rulings, and industry analyses; you may need to interview experts or gather information from clients. Your audience expects you to be the expert on your topic. You need to provide them with the most relevant and reliable information possible.

Assignment: Write a Bibliography

Your team will research your assigned topic and create a bibliography of the sources. This is the basis for your oral presentation. The Bibliography team member is responsible for coordinating this portion of the project, editing and submitting the bibliography.

Each team member needs to find at least three sources. All sources must be from academic or business trade journals. Points will be deducted for any citations from popular sources (*New York Times*, *HuffingtonPost*, etc.). Your team will select MLA or APA citation format and follow it correctly.

The final bibliography will include annotations for each source. The annotation for each source will include 5–8 sentences per source stating the following:

1. Brief summary of the article's information
2. What makes the article unique, compared with other articles
3. How the article will be used in your research project; remember to use concrete details

Sample annotation:
Sandlin, Kathie. "The 7 Deadly Sins of Diversity Recruitment." *The 7 Deadly Sins of Diversity Recruitment.* The Multicultural Advantage, n.d. Web. 28 Feb. 2017.

> This article discusses issues a company may run into while creating a more diversified workplace. It describes a few common mistakes that companies should avoid. The author refers to these mistakes as the "seven deadly sins of diversity recruitment," and they include omission, limitation, imitation, and a few more. Each of these sins, whether they are consciously committed or not, ultimately creates a less diversified work environment. This article is unique because instead of discussing how to create an inclusive workplace, it talks about why a company may not be succeeding in building a diversified business. This article will be used to explain how companies are making efforts to diversify workspaces but are still failing.

Reading 16.2

Annotated Bibliography

Questions about the Annotated Bibliography

By Brock Dethier

1. What are its purposes?

A fundamental purpose of all citation information is to help those who may follow your research trail. Researchers build on other research and rely on previous writers' bibliographic information. By creating any kind of bibliography, you guide readers of your paper to your own sources. By annotating your bibliography, you do a service to your readers: you save them from having to find and skim the source to determine its relevance to their own research question. So a main purpose of an annotated bibliography is to provide readers with a short, informative statement that will help them determine the value of the source for their own work.

Annotating the bibliography also serves important purposes for you, the writer—it helps you remember what was in a particular source. If you include some thoughts on the contribution the source makes to your overall project, you'll soon find that your head is full of ideas about what to write.

2. Who are its audiences?

Whoever has asked you to do the annotated bibliography is, of course, your primary audience, so be very sensitive to the nuances of how that audience introduces the assignment. Ask for examples. Another major audience is you in the future, after you've read scores of other sources and need to find key ideas. As you're studying your sources, think about the kinds of things you want to include in your paper—details, facts, connections to your topic.

Outside of the classroom, other researchers read annotated bibliographies, which can appear in books or on the web. You'll never know who might read them and for what reasons. Because you're writing for such a potentially varied audience, you should probably keep the annotated bibliography formal and to-the-point.

Who was the audience for Anderson's bibliography?

3. What's the typical content?

Summary is the most basic annotation. What is it about? *Assessment* might come in a second sentence or paragraph. Is the source authoritative, recent, well-written? A third sentence or paragraph can focus on its *relevance* to the reader or the writer's work. How does it affect your thinking?

Does each entry in our example have these three parts?

4. How long is it?

An annotation can be as short as a few words of summary ("Freud's thinking on dreams") or assessment ("Outdated") and is unlikely to be longer than a page per entry. The length of the whole document depends on the assignment and the length of the bibliography itself.

5. How is it arranged on the page?

Issues like line spacing and indentation depend on the stylesheet you go by (MLA, APA, Chicago, etc.). But you probably want a heading—Annotated Bibliography, if not something more specific—top and center. Then a space and your first entry—alphabetized by author's last name. Can you improve on our example's layout?

6. What pronouns are used?

You won't see much use of "I" or "you" in an annotated bibliography.

7. What's the tone?

Business-like, formal.

8. How does it vary?

The annotated bibliography is largely an academic genre, and like most academic genres, it varies substantially from discipline to discipline, purpose to purpose. Summary, assessment, and relevance are common elements in annotations, but you should analyze the situation and see what's most useful. Perhaps your readers are interested only in whether a particular source is relevant to other research, in which case all of your annotations should focus on relevance. Maybe your professor wants to make sure that you read the source and will be looking for you to mention keywords or concepts from the source.

Effective Visual Communication

Students are well versed in "death by PowerPoint" presentations. You have been victims and creators of such visual presentations, often since junior high school. With the influence of the popular TED talks and industry experts such as Nancy Duarte and Garr Reynolds, visual communication is changing, and students need to learn effective ways to present information visually. The article you read at the beginning of this chapter, "Why Must I Give a Memorable Presentation?" provides useful information about creating effective visuals.

Applying This Skill: Drawing

In your team, select one student to be the "Reader" for the next activity. The other students will be the artists. Your instructor will distribute paper and markers and the script. The Reader will read a script aloud. The artists will draw the thing described in the script.

Assignment: Create a Visual Presentation

Your team will create presentation visuals to augment your oral presentation. You may use any presentation software of your choosing. The Presentation Visuals team member is responsible for coordinating this portion of the project, editing and submitting the visual portion of the presentation.

Each team member will create slides to accompany his/her portion of the oral presentation.
In addition, the visuals should include:

- A title slide, including names of presenters (in order of presenting)
- Transition slides
- A conclusion slide

A printed copy of the visuals is due in class the day of your presentation. In addition, the Presentation Visuals team member will submit an electronic copy (attachment or link).

Applying This Skill: Rough Draft Visual Presentation Review

Part One: As instructed, develop slides to accompany your portion of the oral presentation. On the day assigned, bring that presentation and a laptop or tablet to class.

Part Two: In your teams, you will review several slide decks via Slideshare.net (see "7 Tips to Create Visual Presentations" by Emiland and "Sample Slides" by Garr Reynolds about creating effective visual presentations). The slide decks are incredibly effective at demonstrating the key principles of effective slide design.

Working in teams, you will apply the principles discussed in the slide decks to your own presentation, discussing examples and ideas for changes to your presentation.

Applying This Skill: Rough Draft Visuals Checklist

Review the visual presentation team members have developed so far. Remember the concepts below. Follow the checklist to ensure the presentation is being developed following best practices.

Rough Draft Visuals Checklist

- **Think Billboards—one idea per slide**
- **Images have Power—images have purpose & meaning**
- **Use Typography**
- **Use Symbols & Creative Data Presentation**

Organization

- ☐ Includes title slide (w/ names) and outline slide
- ☐ Uses transition slides between topics/presenters (sign-posts)
- ☐ Cites sources for graphics/data (ethical use)

Background and Color

- ☐ Avoids busy patterns and backgrounds
- ☐ Color contrasts with text
- ☐ Simple and professional look
- ☐ Uses no more than three colors
- ☐ Uses color for accent/contrast
- ☐ Color use consistent with formality of presentation and topic
- ☐ Consistency between slides

Text

- ☐ Fonts clear and easy to read
- ☐ Text used as headlines (no more than 4 words)
  - o Short, easy to read phrases or single words
  - o Bullets (if used) use parallel construction
  - o Use only key words (remove articles, pronouns etc.)
- ☐ Appropriate font size used
  - o Easy to read (style & size)
  - o Capital letters used correctly
- ☐ Punctuation used correctly and consistently

Arrangement & Images

- ☐ Uses the following arrangement concepts effectively:
  - o Contrast
  - o Unity
  - o Proximity
  - o Hierarchy
  - o Space
  - o Flow
- ☐ Uses meaningful images (not clip art)

FIGURE 16.3 Visuals checklist.

Effective Delivery

As the article at the beginning of this chapter says, "*You* are the presentation." This means you need to prepare, plan, and practice your presentation delivery just as much as you prepare and plan your presentation's content. In the first activity below, you will identify traits and habits that make effective, and ineffective, presenters. Then your team will practice giving your oral presentation together.

Remember to prepare, practice, dress up, and smile!

Applying This Skill: Identifying Delivery Elements

As a team, think about the professors you have that you like and dislike. What makes a professor effective? What makes a professor ineffective? What do you like when professors are teaching? What do you dislike? Make a list of recommendations for professors to increase effective delivery. Be prepared to share and discuss your list with the class.

Develop an Oral Presentation: Developing Effective Delivery

In the theater, movies, and TV, a table read is often the first time an entire cast meets with the director of the production. The cast reads through the script, which allows directors to hear the show out loud. It allows other actors in the show to hear each other, which is also important in group presentations.

As a presenter, you won't stop in the middle of the presentation to say "That doesn't sound right." The table read gives you an opportunity to prepare in a variety of ways, including:

- Hearing the words you've written spoken out loud. The written and spoken word sound very different, so reading your words aloud is essential to creating an oral presentation that flows smoothly and easily.
- Identifying places where the presentation needs more or less information or clarification
- Determining the timing of the presentation: Is it too long? Too short?
- Identifying transitions (between slides and people)
- Seeing how team members (and their pieces of the presentation) work together

In addition, it's your team's first chance to discuss delivery. In an earlier exercise, you identified aspects of delivery that make presenters effective. Now, you can see how you and your teammates speak and sound. Pay attention to the following aspects of vocal variety:

- Tone—monotone, reading, rising and falling intonations
- Volume
- Filler words, such as "um," "ah," and "er"
- Enthusiasm
- Energy
- Smiles
- Determine how all members of the presentation work together

Read the presentation a second time, paying more attention to delivery, including timing, tone, volume, pauses, emphasis, repetition, and rhythm. In your script/notes, indicate places where you want to pause or add emphasis.

Remember, your team succeeds or fails as a whole. You want to provide useful feedback and suggestions for improvement. Be kind, positive, and helpful when delivering your feedback.

A table read is best followed by a formal practice session, during which your team identifies where people will stand and how people will move during the presentation. Actors and professional presenters call the planning of movement and gestures during a presentation blocking.

Your team will want to plan and practice your blocking as well as your delivery. Where will each of you stand when you are speaking and when others are talking? Avoid standing behind the podium, which acts as a barrier between you and the audience. In your practice session, consider how and where to move and stand; this helps avoid pacing and shifting weight, which distract the audience. Provide feedback about how people use their hands, how movement and gesture can add emphasis and impact, and how best to transition between speakers.

Determine how the visual presentation will be advanced. Consider using a handheld clicker so the speaker can advance the slides, or develop a small cue. Avoid a presentation in which the speaker continually says "Next slide" or turns to the person advancing the slides to indicate it's time to change slides.

Finally, discuss your wardrobe. In a business presentation, you are representing yourself, your company, and your brand, and you want to do so in a professional manner. Business professional attire shows respect for your audience, your topic, and your company. Follow suggestions for interview attire as well; avoid anything too tight, too loose, or too low-cut. Be well-groomed; iron your clothes. Wear closed-toed shoes, and polish them. Your appearance is the first thing people will notice, and you want to make a good first impression.

The more you and your team prepare and practice for your oral presentation, the better you will do. Practice on your own. Practice together. Practice often. Your time and effort will pay off in a polished, professional presentation.

Applying This Skill: Table Read

Your team will be given a portion of a class period to conduct a table read of your presentation. This will occur close to the date of the presentation but after you've had time to research and prepare your presentation.

For the table read, you will need to have the notes or script for your portion of the presentation. This requires you to have completed your research and prepared what you plan to say during the presentation. The slides for your portion of the visual presentation should also be nearly complete. Bring a laptop or tablet to make changes as needed.

Your team will sit in a circle. The person to begin the presentation will start. Read the presentation through, focusing on content and transitions. After your first read, discuss what worked well and what you think you can improve.

Applying This Skill: Oral Presentation Review

After presenting and watching other teams present, reflect on how you did. Part of improving is identifying positive and negative aspects of our performance so we can repeat or change the behavior next time.

As a team, answer the following questions. Be prepared to share your answers with the class.

1. What do you think your team did well during the presentation? Why? What would you improve? How?

   _____
   _____
   _____
   _____
   _____
   _____
   _____
   _____
   _____
   _____
   _____

2. Think of the other team presentations. Which ones do you remember? Why?

   _____
   _____
   _____
   _____
   _____
   _____
   _____
   _____
   _____
   _____

3. Reflect on the presentations as a whole. Comment on good and bad aspects of the following: introductions, transitions, and conclusions; delivery, voice (tone, volume, inflection), body language, use of notes, and facing the audience; and visuals.

   _____
   _____
   _____
   _____
   _____
   _____
   _____
   _____
   _____
   _____
   _____

17   Team Project Two: Social Media Audit

In Chapter 10, you learned about writing for the Internet and social media. Please review those principles before beginning this project. In Chapter 15, you also learned about working in teams and assigned each person a team leadership role. Please review those roles before beginning this project. After completing this lesson, you will:

- Demonstrate your ability to assess a project's progress, determine next steps, and relay that information
- Apply best practices for writing social media posts
- Create a document summarizing and presenting information to a client clearly, concisely, and professionally

Assignment: Social Media Audit

Assume your team has been hired by a small or midsized company to perform a social media audit on the company. You will assess the company's social media presence on four platforms and provide recommendations for ways the company may advance its goals.

You will have *two deliverables* for this project: a progress report and a final letter detailing your analysis and suggestions. The tasks and steps are detailed below.

Research:
As a team, select a small or midsized company that interests you. Look at a variety of company websites and social media before determining the company with which you would like to work. The company should have a social media presence but should not have a social media manager.

Determine which social media platforms you will audit for the company. You may select from the following list or propose alternatives:

- Facebook
- Twitter
- LinkedIn
- YouTube
- Google+
- Instagram
- Snap Chat
- Blog

Each team member will focus on *one* social media type and:

- Research best practices for that platform (e.g., what experts say about how to use Twitter for business)
- Research the company's presence (How often does the company post to Facebook? Does it use Instagram?)
- Research 2–3 competitors' presence (How do other companies use the same social media platform?)
- Write/create two or more posts the company could use, following best practices

Your team should develop a marketing theme or campaign (new product, fundraiser, holiday, etc.) for your company. All of your posts will relate to the campaign you develop.

Deliverables:
Each team is responsible for completing two documents:

1. Progress report email
2. Letter to client with social media posts

Applying this Skill: Planning the Social Media Audit and Progress Report

Use the following questions to begin planning for the Social Media Audit. Much of this information will be incorporated into your group's Progress Report.

My group's company is _____

My social media platform is _____

Some best practices for _____ (your social media platform) are:

_____
_____
_____
_____
_____
_____
_____
_____
_____
_____

My company's presence on _____ (your social media platform) is:

_____
_____
_____
_____
_____
_____
_____
_____
_____
_____
_____

Competitors for my company are: 1) _____ 2) _____
3) _____

Competitors' presence on the social media platform is:

_____
_____
_____
_____
_____
_____
_____

Suggestions I have for my company are:

_____
_____
_____
_____
_____
_____
_____
_____

Draft your social media posts here:

_____
_____
_____
_____
_____
_____
_____
_____

Assignment: Progress Report Email

For this assignment, you will write an email reporting on your team's progress regarding the social media audit. You will use the email formatting discussed in class. The Progress Report team member is responsible for coordinating this portion of the project, editing and submitting the progress report.

Progress reports, also called activity or status reports, are common in the business world. They inform a supervisor, coworker, or client about the status of a project. The report may cover a variety of topics, including project design, steps taken, problems faced, monies spent so far, etc. The report also indicates the next steps of the process, including any changes, predictions on timelines for completion, and projected budget going forward.

The progress report for this assignment will identify:

- The company with which you are working and why
- Which social media platforms you are assessing
- Who is assigned to which platform
- Work each team member has completed
- Work each team member has yet to complete and next steps

The progress report should discuss any challenges or problems your team has faced so far and clearly identify steps you plan to take to complete the project by the assigned date. Each team member will contribute a section on his/her progress so far.

The report must include the following:

Introduction
State the purpose of the email and indicate what information will follow in the email.

Body
The following details must be included:

- Requirements of the project (cite/summarize from materials or class discussions)
- Work accomplished and problems encountered (including individual steps and specific details regarding how/when; discussion of problems and how they were overcome)
- Work remaining (including individual steps and specific plans regarding how/when)

Conclusion
Provide an honest overall assessment of your team's progress, including timelines, quality of work, etc. Remember to close by stating whom readers should contact if they have follow-up questions.

The Progress Report

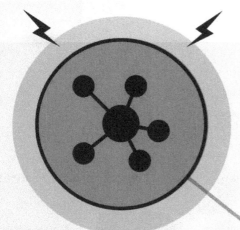

Preparation

This is the first phase when the team reviews the project. What were you asked to do? What have you done so far? What steps will you take next to complete the project on time? Consider any problems/successes you've had so far, how you've overcome them or how you plan to handle them.

Writing

Each team member should write several paragraphs about his/her tasks assigned, steps completed, and next steps. The team lead will compile and proof-read the progress report and review it with the team members. The report should include and introduction and conclusion reminding the reader of the project tasks and deadlines.

Editing

The progress report should have one voice (not sound like several people wrote different paragraphs). All team members should contribute to editing and proofreading the report before submission.

FIGURE 17.1 Progress Report Infographic.

Assignment: Letter to Client and Sample Posts

Your team will write a letter (2–3 pages) as though you are a consulting team presenting a report to your client. You will create at least two sample posts per platform (two Facebook, two Twitter, two Google+, etc., for a total of eight sample posts). The letter should follow the guidelines below and include *an attachment* with your sample posts. The Letter and Posts team members will work together to coordinate this portion of the project, including editing the letter and posts and submitting the final document (letter with posts attached).

Introduction:
- Thank the company for the opportunity to work on the project.
- Acknowledge team members by name (either here or in conclusion).
- Preview the report (outline statement) and transition to body of the letter.

Body:
The body of your letter will include the following information. You should organize the information logically and clearly using sub-headings and visual enhancements.

- Describe your team's process, such as key events, meetings, decisions, problems, and successes, and why you selected this company.
- Identify the company's main goals (either with social media or in general).
- Summarize the company's social media presence (consider using examples of actual posts).
- Assess the company's presence in the market, including comments about competitors.

- Evaluate the company's social media presence, referring to best practices for each social media platform (cite course or research materials).
- Introduce your campaign and how it relates to the company's goals.
- Provide or refer to two or more sample posts per social medial platform; these posts should improve the company's presence on social media, further its goals, and relate to your team's campaign/theme.
- Recommend next steps for the company, referring to research done on best practices.

- Explain how your proposals will help position the company for success.
- Explain how the experience has helped your team members (what have you learned).

Conclusion:
- Express gratitude for the opportunity to participate.
- Refer to team members (if didn't in intro).
- Include contact info.

NOTE: *Only one person, the Letter to Client Team Leader, will write and sign the letter. The other team members will be mentioned by name in the letter. Use the professional business letter format (full block style), including addresses, dates, salutation, and signature. Visual enhancements and even sections/subheads may be appropriate in this letter.*

Sample Posts
After researching the company, its competitors, and best practices, your team will create a campaign or advertising theme (holidays, new product, coupons, etc.). Each person will create at least two sample posts for the

company (for a total of eight sample posts per team) that relate to that theme. For example, if you're researching Facebook, you will create two Facebook posts the company could use.

You will *not* post any of the samples; you will provide them in an attachment to your letter to the client. You will be graded on the quality of the posts and your use of best practices for each platform.

NOTE: Your team may present your findings to the class in an informal presentation during the last week of class.

Sample Posts

Twitter

Post 1:

A big gift in a small package is guaranteed to create big smiles!! Checkout our holiday promotions @ http://schepersjewelers.com/ #Diamonds #Christmas #Gift

Post 2:

CHRISTMAS COUNTDOWN: 20 DAYS!! Have you decided what you want for #Christmas yet? Check out our birthstone pendants and RETWEET THIS POST TO GET 10% off your purchase!! #Gifts #Jewelry #Birthstone

LinkedIn

Post 1:

Do you have a passion for jewelry and design? Looking to change career paths? Need some extra spending cash? Here at Schepers Jewelers, we are always looking for motivated individuals who are passionate about their work. Message us if you are interested in working in a field you love!

Post 2:

Looking for a gift for that special someone this season? Feel free to look no more! Check out this article on all of the fine crafted diamonds and pearls that Schepers Jewelers has to offer! Like and comment below and let us know what you think!

Summing Up Unit IV: Teamwork and Presentations

In Unit IV, you learned a variety of skills employers often identify as ones they look for when hiring new employees and skills that will help you succeed once in a job. Teamwork and leadership are two of the most common skills employers identify as valuable. Once hired, many employees create and delivery presentations, while others are asked to help with social media projects. After completing Unit IV, you should be able to:

- Understand a team leadership role and how to work in a team
- Know how to plan and prepare an oral presentation
- Know how to prepare a visual presentation
- Research a topic using business trade journals
- Identify and use effective elements of oral delivery
- Write a progress report, business letter and social media posts
- Apply best practices for social media and internet writing

Hopefully, the skills learned in this unit will help make you a more attractive job applicant and a more effective employee once you are working.

Conclusion

Communication is vital in any field from finance to accounting, marketing to management and more. Developing or improving communication skills is often a key to getting a job and advancing in the position. You need to know how to present yourself in a professional business environment, how to share your ideas clearly and concisely in effective written communications, and how to tell bosses, colleagues, and clients about projects, proposals, and developments. Knowing how to share your ideas and work with others is essential to your success in the workforce.

The formats you learned—from emails to memos, reports to letters—are a foundation for many business communications. Daily, you will read and respond to emails. Often, you will write memos or letters or reports; you may be asked to conduct primary or secondary research or write for the internet or social media. The foundational writing and communication skills you learned in this course, including the 5 Cs of communication and effective feedback, will help you in many situations.

After completing this course, you have a better understanding of how to prepare and present an oral presentation with visuals, which many people do throughout their careers. You have conducted primary and secondary research and practiced writing for the internet and social media. To prepare for the job search, you have practiced interviewing skills and developed effective resumes, reference sheets and cover letters.

Like most skills, you will need to continue practicing and refining the communication skills you learned in this course. Communication is a continuous process, always changing and shifting depending on the people involved and the situation. You will need to adapt to different audiences and situations, both in your job search and in the workforce. Hopefully, this course has given you a better understanding of the skills you need to effectively communicate in a business environment.

CPSIA information can be obtained
at www.ICGtesting.com
Printed in the USA
LVHW050449301122
734207LV00003B/41

9 781516 591824